BLUE AMBITION

MICHAEL ASHCROFT

BLUE AMBITION

THE UNAUTHORISED BIOGRAPHY OF KEMI BADENOCH

Lord Ashcroft
@LordAshcroft

\B^b\
Biteback Publishing

First published in Great Britain in 2024 by
Biteback Publishing Ltd, London
Copyright © Michael Ashcroft 2024

ISBN 978-1-78590-862-0

10 9 8 7 6 5 4 3 2 1

A CIP catalogue record for this book is available from the British Library.

Set in Minion Pro and Futura

Printed and bound in Great Britain by
CPI Group (UK) Ltd, Croydon CR0 4YY

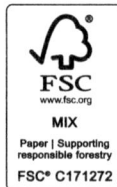

FSC
www.fsc.org
MIX
Paper | Supporting
responsible forestry
FSC® C171272

CONTENTS

AUTHOR'S ROYALTIES

Lord Ashcroft is donating all author's royalties
from *Blue Ambition* to charity.

ACKNOWLEDGEMENTS

M any people kindly agreed to be interviewed for this book and most of them are named in the text. However, some asked not to be identified publicly. They know who they are and I want to express my gratitude to them for providing the various background briefings that proved so useful.

Thanks must also go to the formidable Angela Entwistle and her team, as well as to those at Biteback Publishing who were involved in the production of this book, and to Richard Assheton. And special thanks to my chief researcher, Miles Goslett.

INTRODUCTION

In July 2022, the Conservative Party was in a state of chaos. Having been in government for a dozen turbulent years, its MPs were divided, its identity was confused and its reputation was in the gutter thanks to a series of scandals. Boris Johnson's resignation as Prime Minister that month prompted the third Tory leadership contest in the space of six years.

Of the eight men and women who put themselves forward to succeed Johnson, the Equalities Minister, Kemi Badenoch, was arguably the least well known as far as the public was concerned. She was certainly the candidate whose decision to stand caused the most surprise in Westminster. In the space of just a few weeks, however, she made an impression as a politician with robust views and a strong personality. After seeing off four of her rivals, she was quickly hailed as a rising star. Having survived the race until the fourth ballot, she had cemented her position in the party and marked herself out as a potential future leader.

From September 2022, she served in the Cabinets of Liz Truss and then Rishi Sunak, latterly combining her post as Secretary of

State for Business and Trade with that of Minister for Women and Equalities. This status provided a platform on which to demonstrate her centre-right instincts and, thanks to her trenchant views on questions of race and gender identity, she attracted widespread attention. Significantly, however, it was not only the grassroots members of her party who were interested in her pronouncements but the supporters of other parties as well. They, too, seemed to appreciate that she was prepared to say things that other elected representatives were not.

Badenoch's no-nonsense – sometimes blunt – approach was not the only thing that differentiated her. Her background is also unusual according to the expectations of British politics in general and the Conservative Party in particular. She was born in London but was raised under successive military regimes in Nigeria. She returned to Britain aged sixteen to sit her A-levels and attend university and has described herself as 'to all intents and purposes a first-generation immigrant'. After working as a systems analyst in the banking sector and in a non-editorial role at *The Spectator*, she became a Member of the London Assembly in 2015 and, in 2017, entered the House of Commons as the MP for Saffron Walden.

Having profiled several other MPs in recent years, I was keen to find out what makes Badenoch tick, to establish how she achieved Cabinet rank so quickly, to weigh up whether she has what it takes to become a Tory leader and to consider what the implications for the direction of the party would be if she did. By examining the details of her life and career with the help of some of those who know her best, this book aims to shine a light on each of these areas as the Tory Party grapples with its future direction.

Some people believe that Kemi Badenoch could be the saviour of conservatism in Britain. Readers will be able to judge for themselves how likely this is.

Michael Ashcroft
June 2024

A NOTE ON THE TEXT

I have chosen to refer to Kemi Badenoch as 'Badenoch' throughout this book. Although she used her maiden name, Adegoke, when she stood for Parliament for the first time in 2010, since 2012 she has consistently been referred to by her married name for official purposes.

CHAPTER 1

THE COSBYS

In December 1979, a young husband and wife from Nigeria travelled thousands of miles into the depths of a London winter on a mission to ensure the baby they were expecting could be delivered in what they believed was the best environment money could buy. A few days after a consultation with a Harley Street doctor, they headed south to the suburb of Wimbledon. There, at St Teresa's Maternity Hospital, they waited for the miracle of a new life to begin. At the time St Teresa's, which was run by an order of Roman Catholic nuns called the Sisters of St Anne, was known as a private maternity clinic to the stars. During the 1970s, the children of the media tycoon Rupert Murdoch, the James Bond actor George Lazenby and the Rolling Stones guitarist Mick Taylor were among those born there. On Wednesday 2 January 1980, the name Olukemi Olufunto Adegoke was added to the clinic's record of births. Neither the child's mother, Feyi, nor her father, Femi, could have known it then, but their decision to make the trip to Britain would prove highly significant. For even though the infant was taken straight back home to Lagos to be brought up there, she had acquired a legal right to UK citizenship by virtue of having been born on British soil. Ultimately, this status cleared the path for her to return to London as a teenager in the 1990s, to make a life for herself in this country and, in 2017, to become an MP, which she did under her married name, Kemi Badenoch.

Between the 1960s and the 1980s, it was not unusual for Nigerian women – nor, indeed, those from a range of other countries who could afford the airfare and medical bills – to opt for treatment at the appealingly old-fashioned St Teresa's. It had opened in 1938 as a private hospital for patients with advanced cancer and heart disease, but after the NHS was founded a decade later, it was converted into a small maternity unit. For the next nineteen years, just over half of its seventy or so beds were funded by an NHS contract. This model made it possible for the Sisters of St Anne and their lay colleagues to care for the marginalised in society, to whom they felt a duty, as well as better-off clients who could pay. When the clinic's NHS funding was cancelled in 1967, the nuns were determined to carry on with their work. They did so via a mixture of private patients' fees, donations, bequests and the efforts of volunteers, looking after the needs of as many women as they could, regardless of their financial position. St Teresa's international reputation was well deserved. The standard of care there was so high that between 1948 and 1974, only one mother died in more than 28,000 deliveries. It made a point of not being a conveyer belt-style institution but a place where women were given individual attention and, if they wanted it, time to recuperate in relaxed surroundings after the rigours of childbirth. Badenoch's parents liked the hospital so much they returned there in order that Feyi could give birth to their next child, a son, Folahan, in June 1982. Despite the best efforts of the nuns, however, funding dried up not long afterwards and the hospital was forced to close in

1986. It has since been demolished and a block of flats has been built on its former site.

Kemi Badenoch's birth was formally registered by her mother in the London borough of Merton the day after she was born and it is through the information included on her birth certificate that it is possible to start piecing together her parents' backgrounds and, by extension, some details of her own upbringing. The certificate lists two addresses for Feyi Adegoke. Her British address in January 1980 was given as Flat 31, Ayerst Court, Beaumont Road, Walthamstow, in the outer reaches of north-east London. In fact, this property was where her brother, Emerson Adubifa, and her sister-in-law, Elizabeth, lived. Two weeks after recording the birth with the British authorities, the Adegokes and their newborn daughter were safely installed at the other address on the certificate – their own home, 73 Itire Road in the Lagos district of Surulere.

The Adegokes were an English-speaking couple who belonged to the Yoruba people, a west African ethnic group that makes up about a fifth of the population of Nigeria. Britain first annexed Lagos in the 1860s and from 1914 Nigeria became part of the British Empire, gaining independence in 1960. This meant that Badenoch's parents both grew up in a British colony until they were ten or eleven years old. They had met in the mid-1970s at University College Hospital in Ibadan, the capital city of Oyo state in the south-west of the country. Femi was working there as a houseman, having graduated as a doctor from the University of Lagos in 1974, and his future wife, Feyi, was a postgraduate student specialising in medical physiology.

Although Femi's family were practising Anglicans, his mother, Esther, was born into a Muslim family and by one account lived a rather extraordinary life. She entered into a polygamous marriage as a young woman but left her first husband, who was abusive, and later married Daniel Adegoke, who worked for the Ports Authority as an engineer and draughtsman. They had six children together, one of whom was Femi. She later became a successful trader, dealing in gold and jewellery and selling fabric by the yard from her shop in the largest market in Lagos. She had no formal education and could not read or write, but the wealth she built up from scratch was sufficient to have Femi educated at Ibadan Grammar School, which, like most schools in Nigeria, was fee-paying. Some of her other children attended universities in America.

Badenoch's mother, Feyi, was one of seven children. Her father, Badenoch's grandfather, was the Rev. Emmanuel Adubifa, a Methodist minister. Badenoch is herself a baptised Methodist, though she is no longer religious. The connection between Britain and Nigeria remained strong after independence and Badenoch's parents were both able to travel to the UK when they were university students in the late 1960s and early 1970s. Dr Abiola Tilley Gyado, who knew them both independently, remembers, 'We'd say to each other "Are you going on summer flight?" That meant "Are you going to London?" Students could have holiday jobs in Britain. It was considered acceptable. Kemi's mother and I travelled to London together.'

Femi and Feyi were married in 1977 at Hoare's Memorial Methodist Cathedral in Lagos. By then, Feyi was a lecturer at the University of Lagos's College of Medicine, where she would go on to become a professor of medical physiology. In the early 1980s, Femi decided to open his own private GP's practice, which he combined with working in a teaching hospital. Private healthcare options have always been prevalent in Nigeria because of its underfunded state healthcare service and over time Femi's clinic, which was called Iwosan, meaning 'healing', began to thrive. It was based on the ground floor of 73 Itire Road, which Femi eventually inherited from his mother. The young family lived in the three-bedroom flat upstairs and this was the place Kemi Badenoch called home for the first thirteen years of her life.

After the civil war that had scarred Nigeria in the late 1960s had ended, the 1970s was a boom decade. Lagos, which remained the capital until 1991, was at the centre of this economic upswing. Oil had first been discovered in Nigeria in 1956 and over the next fifteen years production grew steadily to a peak of 2.3 million barrels per day, turning it into the wealthiest and most diverse nation in Africa. Indeed, Nigeria became so prosperous that it was able to export food. Inevitably, the population of Lagos, its largest city, increased at a dizzying rate, from approximately 2.5 million in 1980 to almost 5 million by 1990, as it attracted people from all over the African continent seeking work. Some of the money generated by the oil industry found its way to Badenoch's father's clinic, which secured contracts to treat the employees of various oil companies, and it continued to flow steadily during the earliest years of Badenoch's life. Yet friends say that the Adegokes remained pretty typical among middle-ranking educated Yoruba families living in Lagos at the time, being comfortable rather than truly affluent. There was certainly nothing ostentatious about their life. They had no driver, for instance, though some middle-class families did, and they had no domestic staff either. The children were expected to help their parents keep the house tidy.

Badenoch's father was not the only person in the family who enjoyed professional success during the 1980s. In 1985, her mother, Feyi, was awarded a fellowship to a medical college in Omaha, Nebraska. By then Kemi and Folahan had been joined by a sister, Funlola, born in Lagos in 1984. Feyi and the three children moved to America for almost a year. When they returned to Africa in 1986, it was time for Badenoch to start school. One of the most enduring legacies left by the British in Nigeria is its education system, so much so that even today the two countries are broadly in line with each other when it comes to schooling. Badenoch first went to St Saviour's, a traditional primary school for children up to the age of eleven. Her father had a strong interest in music and enjoyed listening to a wide range of styles, from the Nigerian musician Fela Kútì to Frank Sinatra. In her spare time, he taught her to play the piano. She also enjoyed swimming and reading books written by Enid Blyton, notably the Famous Five and Secret Seven series. As a young girl she was keen on debating, even being asked to take part in a televised children's discussion programme aimed at ten-year-olds. Although she was seen on camera in the studio, she was not asked to participate in the debate, to her annoyance.

If her primary school years were generally straightforward, however, her secondary school career, which began in 1991, was less settled. It opened with a brief spell at the Federal Government Girls' College Sagamu, a state-run boarding school in a rougher town about forty miles north of Lagos. It was one of fourteen federal government colleges established in the newly independent Nigeria with the aim of fostering national unity. Badenoch hated it and left within the space of a year. 'I had a very tough upbringing,' she told the *Evening Standard* of this chapter of her life in 2018.

We all had to do something called 'manual labour'. Mostly it meant getting up at 5 a.m. and cutting grass endlessly. Everyone had their own machete. Because that's how you cut grass in Africa. There were no lawn mowers. We had to tend our own patches. I still feel as if I have got the blisters.

As much as she resented having to do physical work before sunrise, it is just as likely that she felt out of place at the school and missed her parents. By the standards of a patriarchal society such as Nigeria's in the 1980s, her father is said to have taken an unusually modern approach to bringing up his children, often making breakfast for them in the morning and helping them with their homework in the evening. As he lived and worked in the same building, he had more time than many fathers would have done to devote to them and the bond between him and his eldest daughter was always strong.

Having persuaded her parents to withdraw her from her boarding school, Badenoch was next sent to Vivian Fowler Memorial College, a fee-paying Catholic school close to the family home. In 1993, when she was thirteen, the family left 73 Itire Road, which had by then expanded to incorporate an inpatients section and had therefore become a small hospital, and moved to a four-bedroom house not far away in the Gbagada area, where Badenoch's mother still lives. At about the same time, Badenoch switched schools again, this time enrolling at the International School Lagos (ISL), a co-educational college that catered mainly for the children of university staff. It was based within the university campus, had decent facilities and, usefully, its fees were heavily subsidised for the offspring of university employees. When Badenoch arrived, her younger brother was already a pupil there.

In a nation in which it is estimated that at least 500 languages are spoken, English is Nigeria's lingua franca and lessons in every school that Badenoch attended reflected this fact. She communicated with most of her friends and peers in English as well, even though Yoruba was her first language. Indeed, owing to her parents' jobs, her grasp of both spoken and written English was apparently better even than that of some of her teachers. Dr Gyado sent her own children to ISL. 'It was a brilliant school,' she says. 'Kemi was a lot of fun, but she was also inquisitive. She took her studies very seriously. She wasn't very sporty – that may have been because the environment didn't allow it at school. The school was quite academic.'

One friend Badenoch made during her time there was Taiwo Togun. 'We both arrived at ISL in Form 4,' Togun remembers.

Kemi started a few days before me. I met her on my first day. She just came into the class and introduced herself to me. We found out that our parents went to medical school at about the same time, her mum worked in the college of medicine, my mum worked in the college of medicine, so there was a lot in common. She was brilliant in the things she was interested in. She loved English. She was probably one of the best students in our English class. And I think she really liked maths as well. I don't think she had any issues in school academically.

Togun says that Badenoch was not a rebel but she could be outspoken. 'If there was something she didn't agree with, she would respectfully tell the teacher, but I wouldn't call her a rule-breaker,' she says. 'I think her parents probably instilled a certain amount of confidence in her.' As well as being capable in the classroom, she was also a skilled chess player, winning a national girls' competition when she was seven years old. Some might argue that learning chess at a young age would come in useful years later when coping with the political scheming of Westminster, to say nothing of letting her get inside the minds of others. Yet Togun says that at the time they met, Badenoch's ability to checkmate her opponent's king did not simply reflect her enjoyment of the game; it also acted as a unifying force among their year group.

I wouldn't call her a ringleader, but she had friends in all class-es. We had some guys who were the brilliant boys in school and Kemi became their friend by playing chess. I think her dad taught her when she was a child and once the boys became her friend, they became every other person's friend. I think what endeared her to them is she would beat some of them and they thought, 'Who is this girl?!' Sometimes when people are very smart they tend to talk to smart people only, but she broke that idea, so we all became friends – girls and boys, brilliant, average, struggling.

Togun believes that Badenoch's mindset from childhood to the present day has always been: 'I'm probably the best thing in the room, you just don't realise it, and you will realise it sooner or later.' The way Togun describes this attitude is nuanced, however. She doesn't necessarily mean that Badenoch believes herself to be brilliant in all that she does; more that Badenoch feels that her inner strength will eventually come to the fore, an outlook that has helped to bolster the conviction that her parents always encouraged in her. Equally, her instinct to bring people together, which is another form of networking, could be seen as a self-protective measure after the upheaval of being sent away to a boarding school she loathed and which clearly left its mark on her. If this is true, it is a trait that has so far served her well in politics.

During their early teenage years there was a limited amount of socialising outside school hours but, according to Togun, none of the girls in their class had a boyfriend and the idea of hanging around in shopping malls or cafes in the way that, say, European or American children might was absolutely not par for the course in 1990s Lagos. Apart from anything else, many middle-class parents were conservative and quite strict. Badenoch has said that her own family was very close. Unlike the parents of some of her friends, hers remained married, providing a solid platform on which she was able to build. Her family was also fairly relaxed and informal by Nigerian standards and they were apparently known jovially as the Cosbys, after the 1980s American television comedy *The Cosby Show*, whose main character, played by Bill Cosby, was a doctor in New York. Still, there were boundaries that had to be observed. 'I didn't really go to parties,' Togun says.

> Our parents didn't really allow us to go. I don't think Kemi was allowed to go either. Maybe she went to one or two, but her father would be outside, if I remember correctly, or she was only allowed to spend thirty minutes there. Because everyone's parents would say, 'What are thirteen- or fourteen-year-olds doing outside their house in the evening?' From six o'clock, my parents said they didn't allow it, so I don't think Kemi's parents allowed it. It wasn't about security. It was more 'What are you doing? Why do you need to be at a party?' Their attitude was 'That's not what we do. You can wait until university. There's plenty of time to do all of that. Just focus on your schoolwork.'

Badenoch spent quite a bit of her free time with cousins and family friends. 'It was about instilling values,' says Togun. She remembers middle-class life in Lagos thirty years ago as conventional and, like many other cities in developing nations, simpler than it is today. She says that from the age of thirteen, Badenoch lived in what she remembers as being a fairly modest house in a quiet cul-de-sac. It had no garden to speak of. Churchgoing was encouraged and there was little in the way of outside entertainment.

Lots of people had television, but it wasn't broadcast 24/7. It would come on at 4 p.m. and go off at 11 p.m. There were cinemas when my parents were in school, but by the time we were born there were no cinemas until the 2000s, I don't think. I probably didn't see a cinema in Lagos until well after I graduated from university in 2004 or 2005.

Furthermore, people did not tend to go on holiday often and diets were monotonous, consisting mostly of soup and rice. 'Kemi was the first person I met who used to eat wheat bread, or brown bread,' she says. There were few fast-food outlets or anything similar because Western restaurants had not reached Lagos by that point. 'We had Mr Biggs, which used to sell doughnuts, meat pies, sausage rolls, even chicken pie,' says Togun. 'Chicken used to be a luxury then. You only ate chicken once a week.' She adds that most people had to be very careful with their money. 'My parents had to be, and I'm almost certain Kemi's parents had to be because we had similar backgrounds. So you would not get to do a lot of things that you wanted to do, because you had to spread the income you had over three or four children.'

Nigeria has long been regarded as a risky place to visit, but it would probably be difficult for many Britons to grasp just how volatile it could be when Badenoch was growing up there during the final quarter of the twentieth century. It was an era when the country ricocheted from coup to coup, resulting in three decades of military juntas, which were active until the turn of the millennium. Almost nobody was immune to some sort of disruption during this fractured period. Thanks to the near-constant state of economic and political flux, corruption among the top tier of the government and civil service was the rule rather than the exception and the threat of violence hummed menacingly in the background.

In the 1970s, the government had been able to borrow heavily based on its projected petroleum revenues, which by the middle of the decade accounted for almost half of its gross domestic product. President Murtala Muhammed, who took office in July 1975, was in power when some of these loans, which were earmarked for a series of modernising projects, were made. After Muhammed was assassinated in February 1976, General Olusegun Obasanjo succeeded him, serving as Nigeria's head of state until 1979. In that year, Shehu Shagari became Nigeria's first democratically elected president, marking a brief democratic interlude under what became known as the Second Nigerian Republic. Following another coup in 1983, in which the hardline Major-General Muhammadu Buhari was installed as the military head of state, inflation began to soar and living standards fell as the global oil price fluctuated. From the mid-1980s, Nigeria defaulted on its debts and hundreds of thousands of west African economic migrants who had settled there were expelled, in part to ease the job market. In 1986, Nigeria was forced to embark on a structural adjustment programme approved by the International Monetary Fund, necessitating limited public spending and devaluation of the national currency, the naira. By the late 1980s, when Buhari had himself been overthrown by General Ibrahim Babangida, its economy was weighed down by about $30 billion of foreign loans and the World Bank had demoted it to the status of a poor nation. This was the shadow in which Badenoch was raised.

In one sense, growing up under a series of military regimes was second nature to Badenoch, her siblings and her friends. Quite simply, they knew nothing other than the instability under which most Nigerians lived. At the same time, her middle-class family was relatively lucky because they were largely insulated from the disorder. When the value of Nigeria's currency began to drop and exchange rate controls and capital controls were imposed, restrictions were by necessity imposed on family life, but in essence they remained in a reasonable position compared with many of their fellow citizens. With that said, these tensions undoubtedly affected her. In her maiden speech in the House of Commons in 2017, Badenoch spoke of 'living without electricity and doing my homework by candlelight, because the state electricity board could not provide power, and fetching water in heavy, rusty buckets from a borehole a mile away, because the nationalised water company could not get water out of the taps'.

This was not an exaggeration, says Taiwo Togun.

People didn't have generators then the way they do now. If the light went, you had to use candles or lanterns and when there was no light, there would be no water, so you would have to fetch water, sometimes from within the complex, sometimes from the next one. Everybody said, 'The government should do this, the government should do that, why don't we have water, why don't we have light?' Then everybody started providing for themselves, but that didn't start until maybe 2000 or 2001.

It is somehow appropriate to find that, amid the disorder, the schoolgirl Kemi had already become aware of a female leader who had taken a country that was in decline and, through what she called 'the politics of conviction', transformed it. That person was, of course, Margaret Thatcher. In fact, Badenoch has claimed that when she was young, she held Thatcher in such high regard that she would invoke her name during discussions with members of the opposite sex. 'They say a prophet is never loved in their own country,' she told Nick Robinson of the BBC in 2020.

> Growing up in Nigeria – this is a country that is very patriarchal … There were competitions that the girls weren't allowed to take part in because we were girls. There were privileges that the boys were given which we weren't given. And they would laugh at us and say, 'Girls can't do this, girls can't do that.' And you'd just say two words: Margaret Thatcher. And there was nothing they could say in response to that. She was inspirational.

Just how inspirational Thatcher was to Badenoch would become clear, for as Nigeria's economic and political prospects worsened, her parents invited her to help them make a decision that would have profound consequences for her personally. Unbeknown to anybody at the time, the upshot of this was that Badenoch would one day meet Thatcher and, remarkably, would subsequently sit around the same Cabinet table from which her political heroine had run Britain for eleven and a half years.

CHAPTER 2

GOLDEN TICKET

By 1995, Nigeria was widely considered to be a pariah state. Aside from its economy being in the doldrums, human rights abuses were rife and it was rapidly moving up the scale of the most dysfunctional countries in the world. Matters reached a head on 11 November when it was suspended from the Commonwealth following the executions of nine environmental activists who had been incarcerated by the government on contested charges of murder. Among those hanged was Ken Saro-Wiwa, an author who had become one of the regime's fiercest critics. International condemnation followed the killings, with Western nations recalling their ambassadors and the World Bank withdrawing its backing for a multi-million-dollar development deal. Even Robert Mugabe, the corrupt President of Zimbabwe, was critical of Nigeria for having imposed the death penalty so arbitrarily. As Badenoch's parents watched their country sink ever lower, they had begun making plans to remove their eldest daughter from the turmoil so that she could live abroad.

In fact, by the mid-1990s Badenoch's parents were, like much of Nigeria's small but historically prosperous middle class, living in reduced circumstances themselves. Under General Babangida, the head of state, a presidential election had been held in June 1993. Although the result was never officially declared, Chief Moshood Abiola of the Social Democratic Party defeated Bashir Tofa of the National Republican Convention, managing to transcend the complicated politics of ethnicity and religion that had plagued Nigeria up to that point. The majority of voters had been pleased about Abiola's apparent victory, but this outcome appeared to go against Babangida's interests and the poll was annulled. Yet another coup followed in November 1993, in which the merciless kleptocrat General Sani Abacha seized power. All hope of a return to democracy and security was dashed. Instead, the country slid into a long cycle of strikes and protests. Many of these demonstrations took place at universities, including the University of Lagos, where Badenoch's mother worked. It was closed for the best part of a year. Badenoch's father was not immune to professional problems either, as the oil company contracts that had kept his business buoyant for more than a decade were terminated and, in a double blow, many of the nurses who worked at his clinic relocated to Britain and Australia. Money was tight and the future appeared to be bleak. Yet one consequence of Badenoch's parents having grown up in a British colony was that they felt their link with Britain itself was strong. Indeed, it could be said that in some respects they, in common with many other educated Nigerians, viewed Britain almost as an extension of their own country.

'Anyone who had the chance to get out of Nigeria left,' says Feyi Fawehinmi, a distant cousin of Badenoch, of this period.

The economic crisis made life very tough for everyone in the 1990s. People thought it was so bleak and the country had no future. People's circumstances really changed. They didn't take anything for granted any more. You had to fight for everything and rely on friends. Inflation ravaged savings. The damage done in the 1990s destroyed a lot of the Nigerian middle class. Kemi's family was a victim of that. My family was a casualty as well. At that time the greatest love that parents could show their child was to get them out of the country. If you had the means to do it, you would.

It wasn't just the dire economic situation that had an effect on people's outlook. Fawehinmi goes on to say that the sense of lawlessness in Nigeria also hastened many people's departure. 'What was called "jungle justice" was common when we grew up,' he remembers. 'For example, if someone was caught stealing, they might be doused in petrol and set on fire by a vigilante mob. These things have informed who Kemi is.'

Badenoch's 16th birthday fell in January 1996 and she sat the Nigerian curriculum's equivalent of GCSEs at around that time. She also took the SAT exam, a key component in the process of applying to an American university. She has said she achieved a high enough score in it to win a partial scholarship to study medicine at Stanford University in California, but because her parents were unable to afford to send her to America, they decided instead to take advantage of the fact that she had been born in London.

It has been hinted at in some quarters that Badenoch's parents made a conscious decision to have their first two children in Britain not only to guarantee their safe arrival in a reputable hospital but also to secure each of them a British passport. This is a challenging claim which warrants scrutiny. Whenever Badenoch has been asked why she was born in Britain, she has usually explained that her mother had an 'obstetric referral' to a private doctor in Harley

Street and in December 1979 returned to London to give birth at the private St Teresa's clinic. The idea that her parents were NHS 'health tourists' is therefore inaccurate, for no British taxpayers' money was spent on the medical treatment received by her mother. And yet it is the case that anybody born in the UK before 1 January 1983 had an automatic right to a British passport, regardless of their parents' nationality or permanent residence. The question is, therefore, whether Badenoch's parents were aware of this rule when she and her brother Folahan were born in 1980 and 1982 respectively.

As described in the previous chapter, Badenoch's late uncle Emerson – that is, her mother's brother – was already living in London at the time of her birth, and his home address in Walthamstow even features on her birth certificate. But Badenoch has rejected any suggestion that she was what she has called an 'anchor baby', a pejorative term referring to a child who is born to a foreign mother in a country which offers citizenship as a matter of routine. In an interview with *The Times* in February 2024 she said, 'It's very, very aggravating when people say my mother had me here to be an "anchor baby". She's the most incorruptible woman.' Indeed, Badenoch's parents were supposedly unaware that she and her brother were entitled to become UK citizens until this was pointed out to them by a family friend when Badenoch was fourteen years old. On discovering that her parents had applied for a visa to visit London which had apparently been declined, this unnamed friend is said to have explained to them that Badenoch and her brother were technically British on the basis of where they were born and so an application for two passports in their names should be made instead. Badenoch told a 2022 podcast interview with *The Spectator* that her mother found this suggestion 'absolutely preposterous' initially but when she looked into the law and realised there was nothing standing in the way of her first two children exercising this right, the relevant paperwork was completed and dispatched. 'I remember the day that the passports arrived,' Badenoch recalled. 'I always tell people it was like in *Charlie and the Chocolate Factory* when you open the chocolate bar and there's the golden ticket … All of a sudden these pink passports arrived. It was amazing.' According to her, the fact that she was able to assume a British identity at a time of her choosing was down to nothing more than 'fate'. Whatever the truth, it is undeniable that she played no part in deciding where she came into the world and that for her to have been born in London was quite simply her great good fortune.

Badenoch has said that even though she had not lived away from home before, other than for a brief spell at her state-run boarding school when she was eleven, she was desperate to leave the havoc of Nigeria behind. Having grown up in a country where 'tipping' the police simply in order to go about one's daily business was considered normal, the attractions of Britain's liberal society would have been obvious. The idea of beginning a new life in London aged sixteen does not seem to have daunted her in the least, despite the fact she had never even travelled on public transport before. An escape route having been found thanks to Britain's citizenship laws, she and her father made the necessary travel arrangements in the summer of 1996. 'Dad spent several months' pay on my plane ticket,' she recalled in an interview with the *Daily Mail* in 2017. 'We went to the travel agent with all his savings stuffed in a plastic carrier bag. He had £100 left when he'd paid for my ticket, and he gave it to me to take to England. So that's all I had when I arrived.'

Her first port of call in London was 81 Springfield Avenue, a five-bedroom house on the outskirts of Wimbledon. It had been bought not long before by Dr Abiola Tilley Gyado, her parents' longstanding friend who had also been the chief bridesmaid at their wedding. Dr Gyado had been the director of Nigeria's Aids programme during the early 1990s before moving to London to work for the charity Plan International. She had three children who attended boarding schools outside the capital, so she and Badenoch lived together during the week. 'People would talk about people "checking out" of Nigeria,' Dr Gyado says of that period of Nigeria's history. 'That was the language used for those who were leaving. Kemi's parents stayed because they still had things to do there, so she came on her own. She wanted to experience another life. I knew Kemi before she was born. She was like a child to me.' Indeed, Badenoch referred to her as her 'aunt', even though they were not actually related in any way.

Many middle-class parents in Nigeria at that time hoped that their offspring would opt for one of four careers when they grew up: medicine, law, accounting or engineering. Expectations were always high and, as professionals themselves, Badenoch's mother and father were no different. Their desire was that she would eventually read medicine at a British university and, initially, she seems to have gone along with this idea. She quickly set to work finding a suitable school at which to study for her A-levels and settled on Phoenix College, a state-funded sixth-form college for 16–19-year-olds that was within walking distance of Dr Gyado's house. She began there in September 1996. Set in fifteen acres of grounds and with build-ings dating back to the 1930s, it had previously been called Merton Sixth Form College, but its name was changed in 1990 following a reorganisation of the area's secondary education provision. It was underwritten by the Further Education Funding Council for Eng-land, the Department for Education body that was in charge of the sector at the time, and it operated outside local authority control. By the standards of sixth-form colleges in the 1990s, it was considered small, having fewer than 400 students on its roll. Facilities included several tennis courts, a sports hall, a cafeteria, a library and a drama studio. Ultimately it proved unsustainable to run and it closed in 2000 after being in operation for only a decade.

One former member of staff who agreed to be interviewed for the purposes of this book describes it as a happy place, even if it was not at the top of the tree academically. 'There was a fairly low bar to entry – I believe that students needed to have at least four GCSEs at C grade or above,' says this person, who asked not to be named. 'The college wasn't exceptional in any way. There were only between 100 and 150 full-time students in each year and about forty staff.' It is understood that many of the students were there to gain GNVQs or to retake GCSEs rather than to study for A-levels and so class sizes for those, like Badenoch, who wanted to matriculate were small.

According to a prospectus dating from the mid-1990s, students at Phoenix College were encouraged to develop their independence, meaning that the college was in some respects closer in style to a small university than a school. There was no uniform and students and tutors were on first-name terms. 'We offered pastoral support,' explains the former staff member. 'We had a vice-principal who looked after the welfare of the students and every student also had a tutor, but the students only had to be there when they were attending lessons.'

Although Phoenix College appears to have been a neat solution for Badenoch insofar as it was conveniently located for her, and free of charge, her time studying there does not seem to have been entirely without tension. Having grown up in Nigeria's professional middle class, and being used to the rigidity of that country's traditional education system, in which pupils were expected to look smart and behave well at school or face disciplinary action, she seems to have had some difficulty acclimatising to the looser ethos of this particular south London institution. 'What struck me was how foul-mouthed some of the students were,' she told the *Daily Mail* in 2017.

> I'd never used the F-word – my grandfather was a reverend and we were raised as strict Christians – and I found it shocking and scary that young people spoke flippantly, even rudely, to adults. This was an area of London with a large black population, yet it was a black culture I didn't recognise. A lot of damage has been done by accepting this kind of behaviour, shrugging it off as the inevitable corollary of deprivation and poverty.

It wasn't just some of her fellow students who seemed to bother the teenage Badenoch. She also believed that some of the staff were discriminatory. 'Teachers treated us differently from the white people at the college,' she told the *Daily Mail* in 2019.

> They assumed we had it tough. They couldn't tell the difference – and this is where judging by skin colour is a terrible thing – between someone who had perhaps grown up in a very disadvantaged family and had serious challenges, and someone from a stable family who had loads of opportunities. You would have people who quite clearly had special needs – who were autistic, I recognise that now – and it would be like, 'That is just how black people behave.'

Moreover, other members of staff had what she remembers as a depressingly defeatist attitude. She opted to study biology, chemistry and maths at A-level. On the face of it, sufficient grades in these subjects would probably have allowed her to follow in her father's professional footsteps. Since the University of Oxford was, apparently, the only British university she had heard of when she arrived in London, she has said that it was her aim to study medicine there rather than anywhere else. Over the course of the six terms that she worked towards her A-level exams, however, various barriers presented themselves. One story she has told on several occasions is that a senior member of staff at Phoenix College actively steered her away from this aspiration altogether. Having explained that she wanted to be a doctor, and that both of her parents were doctors, she was apparently told, 'Medicine is really, really difficult. Have you considered nursing?' She said that this epitomised 'the culture of low expectations that I've learned, being in the UK'. After this small humiliation, she and a Chinese student went to see another member of staff at the college to seek their advice. As she later told a TED Talk audience:

We both said, 'We want to go to [Oxford] university, what do we do?' And they said, 'There's no point in applying because they'll never take you. They don't take people like you. They're elitist institutions and all they want are posh people, children of their friends and so on. There are many other schools you can go to that'll be just as good.' So I didn't apply [to Oxford] because that's what the teachers told me.

More than twenty-five years after Badenoch left Phoenix College, it would be almost impossible to prove or disprove this account, but the former staff member who agreed to be interviewed says that he is quietly sceptical of it, calling it an anecdote that sounds 'trite'. He goes on: 'I can certainly think of one student who went to Cambridge.' He did go to the trouble of asking a former senior colleague whether they remembered Badenoch, but, like him, they did not. 'If she was quiet and diligent she probably wouldn't have been that memorable,' he concludes. 'We had nice students and nice staff. There was a good relationship between the two.' Dr Gyado offers a slightly different perspective, however. 'Kemi talked to me about the poor behaviour of other students,' she confirms. 'I think we probably arrived at the conclusion that it was because it wasn't a fee-paying school. Fee-paying schools can open up a lot of possibilities.'

Free IT training was also on offer at Phoenix College, which, bearing in mind the internet was in its infancy in the 1990s, was undoubtedly a bonus. Perhaps because of the perceived resistance to her plans to study medicine, or maybe as a result of a growing sense of her own independence, Badenoch changed her mind about her career plans halfway through her A-levels, deciding that she no longer wanted to become a doctor. Instead, she said, she wanted to work in computing. She had apparently begun to learn the art of computer coding at an extraordinarily young age and had always enjoyed problem-solving. She told her parents, with whom she would speak by telephone, and they were disappointed but accepting. The only tasks facing her were to find a computing course at a university that appealed to her and then to secure the requisite A-level grades.

Outside college, Badenoch had to get used to a new way of life. Any pleasure at the freedom she was able to enjoy was interspersed with periods of loneliness. 'Most of the time I was out of the house because I was working,' remembers Dr Gyado. 'I had some responsibilities for health programmes in my organisation so I travelled a lot.' This left Badenoch with time on her hands, sometimes rattling around the house alone, so she took a part-time job preparing food at McDonald's in Wimbledon town centre. Never having eaten a hamburger before, Badenoch couldn't believe her luck in being able to enjoy them free of charge as a perk. 'She worked there at weekends and in the holidays,' Dr Gyado says. 'It wasn't what she had to do. I didn't ask her for money for rent or food. It was her choice to work hard.' With this small income, Badenoch sometimes went out to the theatre. Otherwise she would be at home studying, writing letters to her family, reading or watching television. The idea of frequenting London's pubs and clubs did not occur to her and she had few friends with whom to socialise. 'Her parents came to visit occasionally,' remembers Dr Gyado.

> And we always had ways of entertaining ourselves. Sometimes Kemi would be at home by herself, but there was another girl staying with me – the daughter of another friend. And my children were reasonably close to Kemi. My son was three years older and my daughter two years younger than her.

According to Badenoch's special adviser Daniel El-Gamry, on one occasion when her mother visited, she used the opportunity to do some shopping. 'I've certainly heard Kemi say she can remember her mother coming to see her in London and because inflation in Nigeria was so rampant, she loaded a suitcase with Tesco own-brand rice because it was cheaper to take it back to Lagos than it was to buy it there.'

Having arrived in London in mid-1996, Badenoch did not return to Nigeria for about eighteen months, doing so in order to celebrate her 18th birthday in Lagos in January 1998. She seems to have been an earnest adolescent whose principal focus was her academic work. Pleasing her parents quite naturally mattered to her. But it cannot have been easy to have left them and her two siblings behind in a troubled country while she benefited from a more comfortable life in London, and this chapter of her life seems to have inspired some deep thinking on her part. The generally favourable circumstances she encountered have surely informed her politics and her love for Britain. When looking back on her early years in the UK during a 2017 interview with the *Daily Mail*, she said she thought it was 'amazing, a very special privilege to be a citizen of this country'. She went on: 'Many people use citizenship as an international travel document, but to me it was much more than that. I think of this country with affection, feeling, loyalty. Its values make it special.'

When her A-level results came through in August 1998, she was disappointed, achieving B grades in biology and chemistry and a D in maths. These marks might have been perfectly respectable in the eyes of her tutors at Phoenix College, but they were not good enough to merit a spot at the place she had planned to go on to, the University of Warwick. In view of her parents' assumption that she would go into medicine, it is ironic to consider that these grades would almost certainly not have generated offers from any of Britain's medical schools either, even if she had wanted to attend one of them. She decided not to retake any of her exams and settled instead for her second-choice course, computer systems engineering at the University of Sussex.

Badenoch was quite clear that she did not want to return to her books straight away, however. She decided that she wanted to take a year off before starting her university career. For one thing, her brother, Folahan, had arrived in London that summer. Like her, he moved in with Dr Gyado and was soon studying for his A-levels at Phoenix College, and she wanted to spend some time with him. She also wanted to gain some experience of working in a professional environment. She quit her job at McDonald's and took a summer job in the less fraught atmosphere of the New Look clothes shop in Wimbledon, but she didn't simply want to earn money serving customers all day; she wanted to put her time to good use. She successfully applied for the UK-wide 'Year in Industry' apprenticeship scheme and was offered a berth at an architectural practice called Hunt Thompson Associates, which was based in the north London borough of Camden. Her duties revolved around fixing computers and telephones. She also achieved an NVQ qualification in servicing Apple computers during this time. In 1998, the Labour government had introduced a national minimum wage. It came into force while Badenoch was an apprentice, ensuring her an income of at least £3.20 per hour. According to Dr Gyado, she 'loved' the work and made several friends.

In Nigeria, the political situation had begun to stabilise following the sudden death in June 1998 of the dictator Sani Abacha. Within a few months, General Abdulsalami Abubakar succeeded Abacha as head of state and by 1999 democracy had been restored under the Fourth Nigerian Republic. Yet as concerted efforts were made to repair the damaged country, all was not well for Badenoch's parents. By the late 1990s, her father's clinic had run into such financial difficulties that he was forced to rent it out to other doctors to use. He moved his practice to smaller premises, but eventually the business failed, forcing him to change tack altogether. He invested in some machinery and started a small-scale printing press. Over the next twenty years, he became increasingly politicised himself, rising to become the chairman of a pro-Yoruba group called Voice of Reason. 'Femi's nickname in Yoruba was "Obstinacy", remembers Dr Gyado.

> He was a lovely man and he always encouraged Kemi to ask questions. She was argumentative. She loved discussions. She loved trying to get to the root of things. She was fun as well as inquisitive. I wasn't surprised that she became a politician because she was always able to stand her ground. She is like her father and they were very close.

By the age of eighteen, Badenoch had begun to establish herself in her adopted country, proving that she was serious about making the most of the opportunities that had come her way. As a recent arrival to Britain, she could see its positive attributes very clearly and, indeed, she was a beneficiary of them. Yet there is no mistaking the fact that she also had the ability to view things through the eyes of an outsider, a characteristic that can be extremely useful when it comes to confronting awkward truths and finding solutions to problems. And, as her experience at university would confirm, she was not afraid to challenge those who she felt stepped out of line either morally or politically.

CHAPTER 3

RIGHT-WINGISH

By the time Kemi Badenoch arrived at the University of Sussex in September 1999, its stock was rising. Having been founded only forty years previously, its academic reputation was strengthening and its research facilities were thought to have improved markedly. Studies aside, it had plenty of other qualities to recommend it, which is why its 200-acre campus on the outskirts of Brighton had always attracted a high number of applicants. According to that year's *Sunday Times Good University Guide*, which ranked it the 30th best university in Britain, 'theatrical and artistic entertainments are diverse, clubs and pubs are numerous, and there's even a nudist beach'. With 7,000 undergraduates on its roll, a typical student was described by the newspaper as being 'young, middle-class and from southeast England'. Many people would surely have relished the opportunity to attend such an establishment but, as it turned out, Badenoch was not one of them. In fact, she disliked her time there enormously.

Some will recall the feeling of dread in the pit of their stomach when they began their first term at university, and Badenoch was no exception, for she knew nobody else at Sussex when she arrived.

During her first year she was based in a now-demolished hall of residence in a complex called Park Village. It comprised a series of flats built in the 1960s, each of which accommodated twelve people, who shared a kitchen and bathrooms. Those with first-hand experience of Park Village's unprepossessing living quarters have often complained that each flat lacked any sort of common room or social space of its own, meaning that students would often eat in their bedrooms. For recent arrivals who were shy or reserved, this potentially gloomy set-up could make getting to know their flatmates even more difficult. It was certainly a contrast to Dr Gyado's house, but one consolation for Badenoch was that London was within easy reach by road or rail and, even if she couldn't take refuge in her parents' house, she could at least return to her aunt's whenever she wished. Her brother, Folahan, would also visit her at weekends from time to time.

Her ultimate aim was to attain a master's degree in computer systems engineering, which would require four years' study – and it seems that from her first day she took this task more seriously than any other. Friends say she was bruised by her failure to gain the A-levels she had expected and she was determined not to repeat this mistake. Academic achievement would not only reward the faith that her parents had shown in her; it would also put her on the path to financial security and professional success. With something like twenty-five hours of lectures and tutorials each week, and regular exams to sit, her workload was among the heaviest at Sussex. Yet knuckling down to her books or relaxing in her bedroom was not always possible because of one problem: there was another student who lived in the same flat whose recreational drug use made him volatile and highly disruptive. According to Nkem Ifejika, who was Badenoch's boyfriend during her final two years at Sussex, the flatmate in question was prone to aggressive outbursts. There is no doubt that this complication marred her view of life at university in those early days, but, showing some strength of character, she made it clear that she was not prepared to accept the situation. She was among a cohort of residents who took a stand. Eventually, she alerted the police. Ultimately, their involvement contributed to the drug-addled student's expulsion – but not before his father visited the campus looking for Badenoch in order to try to remonstrate with her. Fortunately for her, she was able to dodge him and no confrontation ever took place. 'It happened before I arrived, but she told me that the student was violent and racist,' says Ifejika.

> He was a north London posh kid who thought he could get away with stuff. I think she got him kicked out of the university. It was difficult for her. It set her back. It affected her work and her grades suffered. I think this situation certainly contributed to her not enjoying her time at Sussex.

Ifejika says that Badenoch always had plenty of opinions when she was at Sussex but she never showed any sustained interest in politics during her student years, either on campus or off it. Bearing in mind the fact that the 2001 general election was held during her second year there, this may surprise some, for it would have been the first British poll in which she was entitled to vote. There was one political issue on which she was prepared to pass comment publicly, however, and it is revealing in its way that she did so not by going on a demonstration or a protest march but by setting out her position in a letter to the student newspaper, *The Badger*.

In the autumn of 1998, an annual higher education means-tested tuition fee of £1,000 had been introduced by Tony Blair's Labour government. This brought to an end the principle of free education for all – one of the key tenets of the welfare state – and it was still hugely contentious a year later when Badenoch began at Sussex. Indeed, this fixed cost remained a major bone of contention around the country, as those who worked in the higher education sector argued with politicians about the damage it could do to equality of opportunity. At the same time, those who were directly affected by the new charge resented having to pay to be at university, especially when their parents' generation had not had this measure inflicted upon them. In fact, within eight weeks of Badenoch becoming a student, the level of anger it continued to generate among students showed itself on her own doorstep. In November 1999, Blair's wife, Cherie, was due to be the guest of honour at a University of Sussex society dinner hosted by the university's chancellor, Richard Atten-borough, but the occasion had to be abandoned after about forty students barricaded themselves into the university's refectory, where the dinner was to be held, and staged a sit-in lasting three hours. As their banners clearly showed, they were protesting against tuition fees and, despite Lord Attenborough using his finest oratorical skills to try to negotiate with them, they refused to leave until they were forced to do so when police arrived and broke up the occupation. It was a small but noteworthy humiliation for the Blairs and it did not escape the attention of the press.

Quite naturally, *The Badger* was among the newspapers which re-ported on this act of rebellion at the time and it continued to focus its editorial gaze on the wider question of tuition fees in subsequent editions. On 18 February 2000, when Badenoch was in her second term, her signed letter to the paper was published. Although it is a slightly rambling piece of writing, its central point challenged the idea that tuition fees were as calamitous a development for students as many people seemed to believe. Instead, it advanced a view that was arguably Thatcherite in perspective, as it pointed out that no individual had a right to expect that their attendance at a university should be underwritten by taxpayers. Rather, Badenoch stated, attending a university was a choice that, ultimately, carried with it personal responsibility.

While this mildly provocative position was likely to have been out of step with many students' thinking on the matter, it confirmed that even aged twenty Badenoch was someone who would not shy away from declaring what she saw as an inconvenient reality, as she opined:

> Some people (not necessarily me) do feel that free education up to A-level is sufficient. And if you cannot afford it, get a loan which you can pay back quickly after you get your wonderful graduate job, and if you still can't get a job good enough to pay back a mere £3,075 of fees then was it really worth it? Let's not forget that there are two sides to every story and why should people who chose not to go to university or whose children are not doing so have to pay taxes for the higher education for the rest of us?

She then seemed to gently mock those who might be inclined to put the rights of minorities above others – in contemporary parlance, her standpoint could be described as anti-woke – as she told readers a little more about herself and her circumstances.

> Okay, so I might be a bit jaded and cynical and from the more insulated parts of this campus (I study Computer Engineering) and a bit more right-wingish, but I must point out that I am a poor, black, female, gay (okay, I'm not but I did think about it

once), disabled if you count the myopia, Christian student. I have also been called 'forrin'. You couldn't get more minority into one person like that if you tried. There must be some non-vocal people out there who agree with me?

Ironically, as her letter stated somewhat obliquely, she did not have to pay for her tuition. The local education authority in the London borough of Merton covered her costs. But in the ensuing edition of the paper there was indeed a letter of approval from a fellow student calling himself 'Dan', who wrote: 'I would like to congratulate [Badenoch] for bothering to express the opinions which I believe are probably shared by a large number of students.' Others were more critical. One, called Phil Lloyd, argued:

The abolition of the grant and the introduction of tuition fees has meant that those students who have not received direct financial support from their parents have to take up part-time jobs during their degree … Their education is likely to be suffering as a result of having to get jobs simultaneously.

Had Badenoch been prepared to respond to Lloyd's point, she would have been able to tell him that she was, in fact, among those who were not able to rely on parental handouts but had to fund herself to a large extent. Her boyfriend, Nkem Ifejika, recounts that she earned whatever money she had by taking on paid jobs.

Kemi worked all the time by temping in Brighton or in London in the holidays. She can type very quickly. It was easy for her to make money and the temping jobs paid quite well. Once she moved to the UK she was self-sufficient. She had very little help from back home because her parents at the time really couldn't afford to help.

Badenoch's independence of thought and her apparent need to make her own way financially in many respects go to the heart of what her university career amounted to, for it is safe to say that she did not fit the mould of the stereotypical student. It seems that her upbringing in dysfunctional Nigeria, and the consequences of her departure to London as a sixteen-year-old, may have had a greater effect on her personality and general outlook than she realised. While she was, judging by her letter in *The Badger*, capable of being witty and irreverent, she was also serious-minded. Ifejika claims that she never prioritised her social life over academic work, she drank alcohol very moderately and she kept herself to herself, even avoiding many of the extracurricular activities that were on offer, with the exception of a brief interest in the Afro-Caribbean Society. She was never at risk of succumbing to the many and varied bohemian pleasures of Brighton and her social circle was small, but she was said to be perfectly at ease with being so self-contained. More than that, however, she had very little time for many of the fashion-conscious and forward-thinking students she did encounter, seemingly regarding them with something close to disdain.

'Sussex had a reputation for being politically active and very left-wing,' says Ifejika.

I remember there was an attempt for some political reason to ban Coca-Cola on campus during our time there. I also remember when student officials banned the *Daily Mail* on campus. I thought, 'You can't dictate what people read!' The Marxist-Leninist Society was very popular. Kemi had strong opinions about how left-wing the students were. She felt that some of them were middle-class and spoiled and didn't understand the real world.

Among the causes in which they are said to have shown an interest was boycotting products made by the food and beverage company Nestlé, on the grounds that it allegedly gave mothers in Africa free baby formula in the hope that, when they subsequently lost the ability to make their own milk, they would then choose to buy formula instead of breastfeeding. 'That was exactly the sort of thing that irritated Kemi,' says Ifejika. 'She found it so patronising. She was a pragmatist. These kids [at Sussex] might have thought they were more African than the Africans who were born and bred on the African continent, judging by the way they behaved.' Indeed, Badenoch herself cited the boycott as one of the issues that drew her to join the Conservatives, telling *The Times*'s Janice Turner in 2024: 'Having parents who were doctors, I knew when women are malnourished, formula milk might be a better alternative, and mothers with Aids can't breastfeed at all. These stupid lefty white kids didn't know what they were talking about. And that instinctively made me think, "These are not my people."'

There was a Conservative society at Sussex, but it was not prominent or popular and Badenoch never got involved in it during the four years she spent there. 'I don't remember her ever saying she wanted to go into politics,' says Ifejika. Yet, taking a longer view, Badenoch has concluded that being at Sussex did inform her politics. 'Sussex was a very left-wing university and if anything probably being there made me more Conservative,' she told a *Spectator* podcast in 2022. 'It was almost a reaction to the very spoiled, entitled, privileged metropolitan elite-in-training at university. I saw it first there.' She went on:

I was just very, very disturbed by those sorts of attitudes that didn't allow Africans agency, and black people in particular, and that's something that has stayed with me for a very long time. I'm very suspicious of a lot of the people who claim to be wanting to help black people or help Africans but really what they're doing is signalling their own status of the kind of person they are but they're not really interested in the people they claim to be trying to help.

While many students regard sharing a privately rented flat or a house as a key part of their university experience, Badenoch shunned the option of living in Brighton and instead chose to stay on campus for her entire university career, relocating for her final two years to a more upmarket hall of residence called Brighthelm. Perhaps the only position of note which she did volunteer to hold during her time at university came during this period when she agreed to be a residential adviser – a head of house-type role in which she was responsible for the welfare of the other students living in the same building.

That move coincided with Ifejika's arrival at Sussex in 2001. Like her, he was born in London but grew up in Nigeria before returning to Britain in the 1990s to finish his schooling and attend university. He began his student days studying engineering at the University of Sunderland but, after realising that he wanted to become a journalist, he transferred to Sussex to study multimedia and digital systems. He was introduced to Badenoch through mutual friends who were not at Sussex shortly before he made the switch. 'We met that summer,' he recalls.

She seemed really bright. One of the things I found striking about her was that I thought she was one of the most intelligent people I'd ever met. We'd play word games and try to see who could come up with a word the other person didn't know the meaning of. One I remember she tested me with was 'sybaritic'. We'd do things like that. She liked to play chess, which her father had taught her. We'd have long conversations. We'd discuss Nigeria, but usually in terms of mutual friends or things we did while we were there.

Badenoch did manage to return home when possible and she apparently threw a small 21st birthday party at the Sheraton Hotel in Ikeja in January 2001, but there is no sense that she ever pined for Nigeria. She and Ifejika remained interested in its politics and current affairs, however. Badenoch could even boast of having a relation in a high place there. Through her mother, she is the first cousin once removed of Yemi Osinbajo, who was at that time Attorney General of Lagos State and who would go on to serve as Nigeria's Vice-President between 2015 and 2023, though Badenoch apparently does not know him well and would never claim to be part of a Nigerian political dynasty. She and Ifejika would follow what was going on in Nigeria, though, specifically when it made international news, as was the case in November 2002 when a fashion journalist called Isioma Daniel wrote an article in the Lagos newspaper *Thisday* about the forthcoming Miss World contest being held in Nigeria. The prospect of scores of women parading on a stage in bikinis had outraged some elements of society, notably practising Muslims, but Daniel inadvertently fanned the flames when she wrote: 'The Muslims thought it was immoral to bring 92 women to Nigeria and ask them to revel in vanity. What would Mohammed think? In all honesty, he would probably have chosen a wife from one of them.' Unwittingly, this remark was the trigger for violent riots in Lagos in which dozens of people died. The newspaper's offices were burned down and Daniel was eventually forced to live in exile in Europe after a fatwa was issued against her.

'I remember we talked about that and Kemi felt strongly that anybody's freedom of speech being curtailed was completely wrong,' Ifejika says. 'We both had strong feelings about things like that, but we didn't spend all of our time talking about Nigeria. One of the things you realise as an immigrant is that it's people that you miss rather than places.'

After they became a couple they had a small number of friends on campus, but it seems that they mainly spent whatever free time they had together. Badenoch was apparently a fan of science fiction novels and the *Lord of the Rings* films. 'She loved Terry Pratchett books,' Ifejika remembers.

And of course she was always very good with computers. She didn't buy off-the-shelf computers; she always built her own. I have a mental picture of her sitting in front of a computer working, usually with a big pack of Haribo Tangfastics or a plate of rice and spicy stew to eat while getting through an assignment.

Badenoch has always been open about the fact that she did not find her course easy. She had to work hard to keep up with some of her peers, but her diligence paid off. She was able to spend eight weeks during her penultimate year on an apprenticeship scheme with a Brighton-based technology firm called Elektro Magnetix. This initiative was organised and run by the Shell Technology Enterprise Programme and her tenure was sponsored by the Department of Trade and Industry. She was paid £165 per week. This experience led to her winning a Sussex Innovation Centre award for overseeing a software development project – exactly the sort of recognition that would stand her in good stead when it came to applying for a job.

By the time she finished her studies at Sussex, she had her sights set on working for a software company. Her specialist skills meant that she was quickly offered a job in London as a consultant at the IT firm Logica, which had a wide range of public sector and private sector clients across Europe. Her salary enabled her to rent her own flat in Raynes Park, just south of Wimbledon, but although she was making decent progress professionally, she soon came to accept that she did not find the work particularly invigorating. Ifejika also began to plough his own furrow, eventually securing a job with the BBC, but they split up. By the time Badenoch was in her mid-twenties, she had begun to find her life in London somewhat stale. A void had opened up and politics would quickly fill it.

CHAPTER 4

ANGRY

On 31 May 2005, the singer and political activist Bob Geldof announced that a series of free concerts would be held in cities across the world in order to raise awareness of global poverty. The project, called Live 8, was conceived as a way of lobbying members of the G8 group of nations immediately before they met for their annual summit, which was being held that year from 6 July at the Gleneagles Hotel in Scotland. Following the concerts in London, Paris, Rome, Berlin, Moscow, Philadelphia, Barrie, Johannesburg and Chiba on 2 July, Geldof said that a report by the Africa Commission outlining a proposal to drop all the debt owed by the world's poorest nations would be presented to world leaders George W. Bush, Tony Blair, Jacques Chirac, Gerhard Schröder, Silvio Berlusconi, Paul Martin, Junichiro Koizumi and Vladimir Putin. This was a key plank of the Make Poverty History campaign, a coalition of aid and development agencies in which Geldof was a leading figure. Having spearheaded the Live Aid benefit concerts of 1985, which had raised more than £100 million for victims of famine in Africa, Geldof called on the public to support his latest cause. 'Charity will never really solve the problems,' he said. 'It is time for justice – and twenty years after Live Aid, people now demand it of these eight men ... What we started twenty years ago is coming to a political point in a few weeks. What we do next is seriously, properly, historically and politically important.'

With many of the world's most popular and successful acts having promised to perform at Live 8, including Coldplay, Paul McCartney, Elton John, Madonna, U2, Stevie Wonder and Pink Floyd, the planned event immediately attracted international attention. Yet amid the excitement, some began to pick holes in Geldof's idea. The BBC broadcaster Andy Kershaw, who had co-presented Live Aid, wrote in *The Independent*:

> I am coming, reluctantly, to the conclusion that Live 8 is as much to do with Geldof showing off his ability to push around presidents and prime ministers as with pointing out the potential of Africa. Indeed, Geldof appears not to be interested in Africa's strengths, only in an Africa on its knees.

A campaign group called Black Information Link decried the lineup that would be playing at the London concert as 'hideously white' because only one of the twenty-two performers, Mariah Carey, was from an ethnic minority background. And some black musicians joined the chorus of naysayers, including the Senegalese singer Baaba Maal, who said, 'I do feel it's very patronising as an African artist that more of us aren't involved. If African artists aren't given a chance, how are they going to sell records and take the message back to Africa?' A spokesman for the organisers of Live 8 claimed that several black artists had been asked to take part but were unavailable. He added that an insufficient number of black British musicians were well-known enough to secure a global audience.

Fearing a backlash, however, Ms Dynamite, Snoop Dogg and Youssou N'Dour were rapidly added to the bill in London in order to make it more diverse. Yet for many, this did not go far enough, and so a further compromise was reached. In the middle of June, it was announced that a special free show featuring only African musicians would be added to the Live 8 roster. It was to be called Africa Calling and it would be held at the Eden Project, the botanical garden in Cornwall. Although it was never broadcast on mainstream television along with the rest of Live 8, it was available to watch on a BBC digital channel.

In the short term, Live 8 was considered a success. Aside from the concerts being enjoyed by millions of people around the world, G8 leaders agreed to double the amount given by them to the poorest nations by 2010, boosting the annual aid package to $50 billion annually. In conjunction with the IMF, the World Bank and the African Development Bank, the amounts owed by eighteen of the most 'heavily indebted poor countries' were cut altogether. And another twenty countries were also eligible for debt relief. There is some doubt as to whether every aspect of these pledges was ultimately honoured within the timetable set out, but the impact of the initiative was vast. That summer, the white wristband bearing the logo 'Make Poverty History' that was produced in aid of the cause was worn by an estimated 8 million people in Britain alone.

One person who paid attention as the various Live 8 plans were announced was Kemi Badenoch. She grew increasingly irate as she did so. Prior to Live 8, she had attended the annual Hay Festival of Literature and Arts in Hay-on-Wye in Wales. There, she listened to distinguished figures speaking in sweeping terms about the plight of ethnic minorities suffering from institutional racism. Their attitude needled her and she had begun to immerse herself in the works of the black American economist and philosopher Thomas Sowell, whose conservative views make him a fierce critic of ideas such as positive discrimination and racial quotas. 'When people get used to preferential treatment, equal treatment seems like discrimination' is one of Sowell's many memorable aphorisms. Taking into account Badenoch's own forthright approach to politics, it is not difficult to accept that Sowell's thinking must have influenced her quickly. She has said she felt it condescending that wealthy Western musicians like Geldof had taken it upon themselves to speak on behalf of African people in order to tell world leaders what Africa needed. Furthermore, she was incredulous at the idea that African musicians were only belatedly invited to join the project and were then seemingly relegated to a venue hundreds of miles from London instead of being able to perform at Hyde Park along with the principal bands and singers. In a speech she gave in 2011 in which she touched on these issues, she asked the audience, 'Who would ever call [Nigerian singer] D'banj to come and speak to Tony Blair and tell him exactly what he needs to do in the UK to make it a better country? They'd never do that, and yet the reverse happens.' She added, 'And then they had the African bit in [Cornwall] where all the African musicians went. Nobody watched their bit. It wasn't part of the main show.'

Having determined in her own mind that African people had been forced to assume second-class status in every aspect of Live 8, she told her audience that the irritation she felt about it led her to make a decision. 'The reason why I went into politics was because I was angry. I was a very angry young person. I was angry about so much stuff. And two things that really, really got my goat were education and international development.' Realising that she had the time to devote to pursuing a political career, she decided, aged twenty-five, to join the party with which she felt most naturally aligned: the Conservatives. She has since said that 'in joining the party I felt like I had found my second family'.

At that time, the Conservative Party was on the cusp of fundamental change. The Labour Party under Tony Blair had won its third consecutive general election in early May 2005, prompting the Tory leader, Michael Howard, to resign. He promised to stay in post until his successor had been voted in by party members. In order to ensure that a wide range of candidates had time to consider their options, he put in place a protracted timetable. Nominations opened in early October and the result would be declared in the first week of December. This meant that a good deal of the political discussion in Britain in the interim revolved around the question of who would take on the mantle from Howard.

The perception that the Tories were old-fashioned and out of touch when compared with New Labour had never really been shaken off under any of the four leaders who had succeeded Margaret Thatcher. Howard, as the last member of that electorally unsuccessful quartet, was persuaded that a fresh approach was needed if his party was to achieve power again. With this in mind, he resolved that one longstanding MP and potential inheritor of the crown, David Davis, should not triumph. He formed the opinion that if Davis were leader, the party would drift rightwards and would then face certain defeat at the polls. Seizing the initiative, Howard quickly put down a marker by appointing the left-leaning moderniser Francis Maude as the new Conservative Party chairman. He then promoted two of his brightest young MPs, George Osborne and David Cameron, to the key posts of shadow Chancellor and shadow Education Secretary. Wanting his legacy to be victory at the next general election, Howard soon came to believe that the 38-year-old political centrist Cameron was the party's greatest hope. Ultimately, four MPs entered the 2005 Conservative leadership race – Kenneth Clarke, Liam Fox, Davis and Cameron. It was Davis and Cameron who advanced to the final stage and, on 6 December, Cameron was declared the winner, having gained more than twice as much support from the party's national membership as Davis.

Badenoch's own political calling coincided with this contest. She has said that before she became a fully paid-up member of the Conservative Party she sought the advice of a black friend who worked for the law firm Clifford Chance and who was involved in overseeing a scheme that helped young ethnic minority people into jobs in so-called magic circle law firms in the City of London. His response to the idea was apparently frosty. He told Badenoch that he believed the Conservative Party was both racist and elitist. Yet by casting these aspersions, he reminded her of nobody so much as the Phoenix College tutor who, several years previously, had advised her against trying for the University of Oxford for the same reason: that it was not an institution for people like her. This time, she realised that she owed it to herself to establish the truth independently. She paid her fee and became one of the party's 253,000 members.

In many ways, her timing was impeccable. Within the space of a few months she was invited to a Christmas party in London organised by Conservative Future (CF), the youth wing of the party that was open to those aged thirty and under. Cameron's recent leadership victory ensured the mood was high. With the modernisation mantra ringing in everybody's ears, there was a collective feeling that for the first time in almost a decade the Conservatives had received the jump-start that would enable them to compete with Labour on even terms. Badenoch was keen to become actively involved in this exciting new project and that night had the good fortune to strike up conversation with another guest, the future Tory MP Conor Burns. 'I was a vice-president of CF and I got chatting to this casually dressed young lady and I was immediately struck by her personality,' Burns recalls.

> She didn't seem to know anybody there and I said something to her and she disagreed with me and we then began a lively discussion and she just seemed really gutsy and I was very taken with this. I introduced her to a few people and the following day I emailed Francis Maude and I said, 'I think you should get her in and get her onto the candidates list because she's the future of the party.'

Maude's recollection is slightly different.

> I first met Kemi at a Conservative Party event in south London, though whether it took place before or after Conor emailed me I cannot remember. I was there as party chairman and it was at a time when I'd been urging the party that we needed to become much more representative and diverse in terms of our parliamentary candidates. Here was this very impressive young woman and we were talking and she said, 'I'm really interested in politics, what should I do?' and I said, 'Of course you should be an MP.' And she was a bit taken aback by that because I don't think it had occurred to her that she might try to stand for Parliament, but I encouraged her to apply to go on the candidates list.

A more formal meeting then took place during which Maude suggested to Badenoch that she might like to join the Globalisation and Global Poverty Policy Group, which was in the process of being set up by David Cameron. 'She made such an impression on me when we met,' Maude adds. 'She was very bright and articulate and there was no bogus humility, no nonsense. She had self-belief without being cocky.'

The wheels seemed to turn with impressive speed for Badenoch. Cameron was in fact trying to get six new policy groups up and running at that point, which had the aim of reassessing, over an eighteen-month period, the Tory strategy on issues ranging from social justice to the environment. Each was led by a senior Conservative who had been instructed by Cameron to 'think the unthinkable' in his quest to pursue what he called 'compassionate Conservatism'. The global policy group was to be chaired by the senior backbencher Peter Lilley, who before entering Parliament in 1983 had been an economic consultant on aid and development in Africa and Asia. Cameron regarded redefining the party's global goals as crucial to his modernisation project, declaring that fighting global poverty was one of his top priorities. In fact, the first spending commitment the Conservative shadow Cabinet made under his leadership was to increase Britain's international aid contributions to 0.7 per cent of national income per year. Badenoch was invited to an interview with Lilley and, after scanning her CV, he offered her a part-time voluntary role which began in early 2006. At about the same time, the Tories surprised many on the left by announcing that Bob Geldof would advise the global group on a non-partisan basis. This meant that, somewhat ironically, the man whose apparently patronising stance on tackling African poverty had contributed to Badenoch joining the Conservative Party in the first place would be attached to the same project as her.

Cameron's success in persuading Geldof to work with his party was seen as a feather in the new leader's cap and, given Geldof's historically strong relationship with Tony Blair, the singer's association with the Conservatives was considered a crucial way of showing voters that the party was changing. There was no way Badenoch would have jeopardised the advance she had already made personally by withdrawing her services from the project as a result of Geldof's involvement, but she has said subsequently that she found him 'rude'. One member of the policy group says Geldof was 'a figurehead more than anything else' and is chiefly remembered for his colourful language. 'Bob only turned up to a few meetings,' says this person, who asked to remain anonymous.

> But he was unbelievably rude to everybody and he swore a great
> deal about everything. I remember once someone had bought
> a piece of jewellery during a working trip to Tanzania and Bob
> asked what it was and he said – in no uncertain terms – that they
> shouldn't have bought it. He barely contributed to the final report.
> I only remember him speaking once or twice. He wasn't the most
> helpful when he was with us all. I think that's what Kemi's prob-
> ably referring to. It wasn't that he had anything against her in
> particular.

The project was divided into eight working groups: aid, conflict, corruption and governance, the Department for International Development (DfID), economic development, micro-finance and entreprencurship, trade and China. Badenoch was mostly involved in the trade group. Part of her brief required her to review policy ideas that were sent in. Reaching back almost twenty years, Lilley says she also worked on planning and organising.

When she volunteered to help, she was running the IT system of a bank and she offered to create a knowledge management system to handle all the information we would be garnering. But it soon became apparent that she was worth having as a full member of the commission. So she'd come to the monthly meetings. She was young, but I don't recall her being presumptuous. Everybody was pretty outspoken. We'd go round the table and people would give their views. She doesn't stick in my memory as speaking over the top of everybody or as being silent. She was the same as everybody else.

Badenoch has claimed that one measure she pushed for during these meetings was the merger of the Department for International Development, which was created in 1997 during Tony Blair's first term, with the Foreign Office. This finally came to pass in 2020, under Boris Johnson. 'Everyone in the room laughed at me [when I suggested it] and look where we are now,' she told Nick Robinson of the BBC in 2020. 'So I feel vindicated fifteen years later that what I said we should do has finally been done.'

During one of the team's fieldwork trips to Nigeria, Badenoch, who met them in her home country, proved her worth in several ways. 'We spent a few days in Ghana and then a few days in Nigeria,' Lilley says.

While we were in Ghana we told people we were going to Lagos and they raised their eyebrows. We were so busy, I didn't have time to think about this until we got on the plane and I said to Lisa Hayley-Jones, the director of the project, 'Are we going to be safe?' and Lisa said, 'Yes, thanks to Kemi we've organised two Land Rovers – one for us and one for the armed guards.' So we had armed support because getting from the airport to the main area you had to go past police and army barracks and we were warned that rogue policemen and rogue soldiers would occasionally stop vehicles and demand money with menaces.

Lilley also calls to mind meeting Badenoch's parents in Lagos. 'They were charming, gentle people,' he says.

Both of them were academically distinguished. They said to me, 'Look after our daughter, won't you?' Kemi told me the next day they were worried about her going up to the north of the country because, they warned her, probably tongue in cheek: 'They eat people like us up there!' She explained that this was because her family was from a different tribe. She thought it was very funny. I don't know to what extent she was being serious or just exaggerating their concern. But we went up to Abuja and we were looking at various aid projects organised by the Department for International Development. One was about teaching the 'market mammas', the businesswomen in the city, who were illiterate, to write business plans. And during the meeting Kemi leant forward and said, 'If they're illiterate, how can they write business plans?' And you could see a bemused look on the faces of the DfID officials, who really hadn't thought about this fairly fundamental problem. The rest of us had been too bashful to ask, but Kemi asked this very sensible question. I remember she was good throughout at asking pertinent questions.

Lisa Hayley-Jones backs this up.

Kemi was part of the globalisation and poverty group visit to Nigeria looking at aid and trade. She was able to set out the cultural and political background of the country to help us understand how it operated, which was so useful for our report. Obviously Kemi's upbringing in Nigeria helped enormously.

In June 2006, Lilley's twenty-strong group produced the first stage of its report. It was presented by David Cameron at Oxford Town Hall at an event held in conjunction with the charity Oxfam. Badenoch was also there and, according to her, the evening took a rather surreal turn as far as she was concerned. At one point during Cameron's speech, a sandal-wearing middle-aged white woman sitting in the audience tried to challenge him. She is said to have claimed that as a white man from a privileged background he could not possibly have sufficient understanding of the plight of the poor in Africa or of how best to tackle Africa's debt problems. In some respects it sounds as though this woman's point was not entirely dissimilar to Badenoch's own position vis-à-vis the previous year's Live 8 concerts, in which she had taken a critical view of Bob Geldof. When Cameron's speech ended, however, Badenoch decided to go and speak to her in order to persuade her that Cameron was a man of integrity who genuinely wanted to make a positive contribution to the issue of world aid. If nothing else, she felt qualified to do so because she had assisted with the report under discussion, proving that Cameron was not trying to claim that he was able to solve Africa's problems on his own.

When Badenoch introduced herself as a member of the Conservative Party, and as part of Cameron's foreign aid policy review team, the woman is said to have stared back at her in disbelief and then lambasted her for being a Conservative before suggesting that she was too wealthy and too immature to understand the world.

Irritated by the verbal jabs to which she was subjected, Badenoch accused the woman of not really being interested in helping black people but rather using them as a weapon to fight her own enemy. Apparently, the woman, whom Badenoch quickly realised 'had issues that have nothing to do with Africa', slapped her in the face and then ran off. Badenoch gave chase. 'By this time everyone was looking,' she recalled in a 2011 TED Talk.

> She got to the top of the stairs and I caught her by the hair and I pulled her back and then I just realised the whole room had gone silent. Most people would not have seen the slap. What they would have seen was a 26-year-old black girl holding this old white woman, looking like she was about to beat her, and I just thought, 'Oh my god!' She ran out of Oxford Town Hall and I never saw her again, thank goodness.

There is more than a hint of suspicion among some of Badenoch's friends that she may have embroidered this tale as she told it a few years later, but however faithful to the truth her account was, no harm was done to her political prospects because of the contretemps. She carried on working under Lilley in her part-time role, combining it with a change in her professional career. Having grown bored of the functional post in which she served at Logica, in June 2006 she secured a new berth as a business and systems analyst with the Royal Bank of Scotland, leaving that post three months before the bank crashed in the financial crisis of 2008, requiring a £45 billion taxpayer-funded bailout. Alongside these commitments, she had also embarked on a part-time law degree at Birkbeck College in London, which she completed in 2009. According to friends, she wanted to understand the law better in preparation for the day when she might become an MP and, therefore, a legislator. This confirms that she took Francis Maude at his word and intended to pursue a career on the national political front line, despite not even having any experience of local politics by this point.

'She came to the policy group meetings when she could as she was working full-time,' says its director, Lisa Hayley-Jones.

> She was pretty new to the political field. I'd been involved in politics most of my working life. When we chatted it was obvious she was very bright and determined and could go far in whatever career she chose. She was very interested in what was going on politically. She made no secret of the fact she wanted to be an MP. Two other future MPs, Neil O'Brien and Alan Mak, were also on the team. It was already clear to me that she was going to dedicate herself to politics. Others sometimes get involved in the political world by accident but Kemi knew what she wanted to achieve and wanted to give it 110 per cent and make a difference.

As a young, black, female member of the Tory Party in the early part of the twenty-first century, Badenoch was considered unusual enough to be noticed. Some who worked in Fleet Street wanted to know more about her and in December 2006 she was asked to give a short interview to *The Observer*'s magazine as part of a wider feature it ran on the Conservatives' fortunes. In the piece, she was effusive in her praise for the direction of the party under David Cameron, shooting down the notion that it was an organisation for wealthy, anti-immigrant voters and pointing out that since becoming a Conservative member she had met more openly gay people than ever before. She acknowledged that as a black woman she 'may not fit the image of a stereotypical Conservative', but, in an early sign that her instinct was to reject identity politics, she dealt with this question rather neatly by adding simply, '…we really don't have a one-size-fits-all stereotype'. She went on:

> I'm not one of those Conservatives who thinks every problem in the country is down to Blair and the Labour Party. I just believe that the Conservatives would do a much better job of running the country. What's special about Cameron isn't his changing the party but his ability to demonstrate the way it already has changed and highlight some of the great things we care about which many people are unaware of.

Some who were close to her took a bit more persuading, however. Her Labour-supporting brother, Folahan, who shared a flat with her, says he was 'very surprised' by her commitment to the Tories. 'She once asked me why I supported Labour,' he recalls.

> [I told her] they were seemingly immigration friendly and it seemed to be what ethnic people are supposed to do. I can't re-member much of the rest of the conversation, but I remember she spoke passionately and convincingly about the 'opposition' party and I became open-minded and for the first time actually started listening to what Conservatives had to say.

The varied portfolio of interests that she pursued undoubtedly placed a heavy demand on her time, but as a single woman in her twenties, she knew that if her political dreams were to be realised, there might never be a better opportunity to get into politics. 'She wasn't as able to devote as much time to the policy group as the others,' concedes Hayley-Jones.

> But she did what she could. I seem to remember she wasn't allowed to have her mobile phone switched on at work, so she was obviously very busy in her day job. Between her, Alan Mak and Neil O'Brien, she was probably the least politically experienced, but they were all clever and you knew they were going to get somewhere.

Being in the policy review group brought her into contact with figures from whom she could learn and who might one day be able to help her future career. This idea is borne out in the final 500-page report, 'In it together: the attack on global poverty', which Lilley produced. When it was submitted to the shadow Cabinet in the middle of 2007, Badenoch's name appeared at the back of it alongside the other contributors, who included the sitting Conservative MP Ed Vaizey and the future chief medical officer for England Chris Whitty. As shall become clear, it wasn't just Peter Lilley who would assist her later on but also Alex Morton, who served as the secretary to the policy group, and Neil O'Brien. 'It was a very good launch pad for her,' says Hayley-Jones.

> The report gained a lot of attention. It gave Kemi a foundation in politics and showed her how to deal in the world of politics and policy research. We presented the report to David Cameron, so all of this gave her a good grounding in what frontline politics is like and an understanding of how parties and people and egos work.

Badenoch's fortuitous meetings with Conor Burns and Francis Maude opened a door for her. But her fixed opinions and naturally tough character, coupled with her ability to see that things could and should be done differently, gave her the confidence to walk through that door by joining Lilley's policy group. By 2007, she was ready to continue to the next phase of her political career, but it is noteworthy that some who knew her then say that she has changed in the intervening years. One commented, 'She's definitely hardened since then. Some of the Kemi that I remember I don't see now. There used to be a lot more laughter from her. But of course, she was in her twenties at that time and I suppose she had a different outlook on life.'

CHAPTER 5

NEXT STEPS

Within a week of David Cameron's election as Tory leader in December 2005, he announced that the existing selection of Conservative candidates wanting to stand for a seat at Westminster would be frozen and a new 'A-list' of applicants would be introduced instead. Theresa May, who was then a member of the shadow Cabinet, is remembered as having been at the forefront of driving this initiative, which was also known as the priority list. Its aim was to encourage an equal number of men and women to stand in winnable parliamentary seats. A handful of Conservative Party stalwarts, including Ann Widdecombe, railed against what they saw as the imposition of positive discrimination in favour of women, but Cameron was committed to the plan. If the Conservatives were to govern, he believed, they had to reflect the make-up of the country. Within six months, party chiefs had selected about 100 A-listers who were able to start seeking possible seats around the country in preparation for the next election, which had to be held by the spring of 2010.

Tory MPs were not the only ones to find the A-list scheme contentious. Many local associations found that they were put under pressure to relinquish the exclusive power they had previously enjoyed to select their own candidates. Furthermore, some white middle-class men who in previous times might have been short-listed felt that they were suddenly at a disadvantage. This fuelled suspicions that identity politics was taking root in the Conservative Party. When Badenoch first began to think about putting herself forward to fight a parliamentary seat in 2006, some senior Tory figures were so determined to promote aspiring MPs who embodied its transformation into a political force that was fit for 21st-century Britain that her status as a young black woman might have made her seem like prime A-list material. Yet as a student of Thomas Sowell, she never had any truck with quota systems or affirmative action, believing that all prospective MPs should earn their place in the Commons through merit alone. If she ever was offered a place on the A-list, she did not take it up.

In May 2007, she took her first step onto the property ladder, buying a flat in Brixton, south London, for £80,000 with a mortgage. This ground-floor apartment was in a new complex at 37 Effra Parade. The developer granted a lease of the block to Family Mosaic, a housing association, which in turn made the flat available to Badenoch under a shared ownership scheme. Land Registry documents show the flat was valued at £320,000, meaning that Badenoch bought a quarter share. She paid £6,000 a year in rent to Family Mosaic on the remainder, with the option of buying the property outright later at the going rate. (In fact, she sold her quarter share in 2016 for £125,000.) Her brother, Folahan, lived there with her for a period of time. In the summer of 2008, she began a new job as a systems analyst at the private bank Coutts, which had been bought by the Royal Bank of Scotland in 2000. Although she stayed at Coutts for the next seven years, she found the work frustratingly bureaucratic. She was able to see beyond it, however, for like many aspiring politicians she also took on some voluntary roles in her local area, serving as a governor simultaneously at the Jubilee Primary School in Tulse Hill and at the St Thomas the Apostle College in Peckham, as well as teaching chess to pupils at the Bishop Challoner School for Girls in Tower Hamlets whenever time allowed. For eight years, from 2008, she was also a non-executive director of the Charlton Triangle housing association, part of the Family Mosaic group from which she had bought her flat.

There was one activity that trumped all of these commitments, however. Soon after moving to Brixton, she joined the Dulwich and West Norwood Conservative Association. Despite being close to central London, where the Conservatives had historically been less popular than the Labour Party, it had a busy, committed and purposeful membership. This included six councillors who belonged to Lambeth Council and six more who sat on Southwark Council, the two London boroughs that straddled the local parliamentary constituency. 'It wasn't like some associations which consist of one man and a dog,' says the former association chairman Russell A'Court. 'It was a very active and a very political association. When Kemi came, she impressed us. She was personable, she had a good sense of humour, she was capable of being challenging in conversation and she was an interesting person.' She was quickly asked to be a deputy chairman of the association and given what was regarded as the unenviable post of membership secretary. 'That's a hard role to fill because it's not very exciting and it's difficult trying to find new members. Most people would rather take on the political role, which covers all the campaigning stuff. But we persuaded her to do the membership role,' A'Court adds.

In common with Conservative associations in scores of others seats across the country, by late 2007 Dulwich and West Norwood was beginning to turn its attention to the next general election. As a result of Cameron's modernisation programme, pressure was being brought to bear in that part of south London on what kind of people should be chosen. 'Our association was not typical,' says A'Court.

> It was passionately pro-Cameron and his style of politics, but we were used to fighting areas that were hostile to the Tory Party in London. We shared his view that the party needed a more diverse range of people standing for Parliament, but this was not the only criterion when we were choosing our own candidate.

As a result, there was what A'Court describes as 'a bit of a tussle' in the lead-up to the selection. 'CCHQ basically wanted to impose candidates on us and we fought back very hard on this because we wanted to make our own selection.' The figure delivering these orders was John Maples, the deputy chairman of the Conservative Party with responsibility for candidate selection. Some found it ironic that Maples was pressing the case for diversity given that he himself was a middle-aged white man who was the product of Marlborough College and the University of Cambridge. When he had been chosen to fight the south London seat of Lewisham West at the 1983 general election, the year that he first entered Parliament, his selection had been based on nothing more than his ability and his appeal to the local party. A quarter of a century later, he was foisting new terms of trade upon associations and there is little doubt that he was seen by some to be trampling on constituency autonomy.

Russell A'Court and the chairmen of ten neighbouring associations decided to meet Maples. In what sounds very much like a settlement, it was agreed between them that a pool of aspiring MPs covering the whole of inner south London should be created. From this group, selections could be made. 'I told John I thought we'd get the outcome he wanted but that the associations would have a say in it. In other words, it was a compromise,' A'Court recalls. During the summer of 2008, the eleven associations formed what came to be known as the 'south London tranche'. Thirty-two names were compiled, split evenly between the sexes, and each association chose a longlist from the tranche, who were then interviewed. 'Dulwich and West Norwood was the first association to select a candidate and Kemi was among the names, so we shortlisted her, noting that she was the only candidate local to us at the time,' explains A'Court.

> I hadn't clocked previously that she was on the candidates list. Lots of local activists were on it, but I hadn't realised she was. She hadn't been around for long. She certainly hadn't tried for a parliamentary seat before. She wasn't well known in the association at that time. She was a fairly new member. I didn't think she was going to be outstanding, but we invited her for an interview.

He is sure that Badenoch was only ever on the standard Tory candidates list as opposed to the A-list.

The agreed format was that each person would deliver a short speech to the executive committee and then answer questions. Following this, the four candidates whom the committee considered to be the best performers would advance to the second round, in which the membership would be able to vote for their preferred choice. 'Kemi didn't really get the tone of her speech right,' remembers A'Court of the executive committee meeting.

> It wasn't the best speech. But I noticed that when she came to

answer questions, she really opened up. She was articulate and had a very good understanding of the issues. When she wasn't reading from a script she could convey a sense of conviction and you really got the impression she'd thought about what she was discussing. We hadn't realised just how effective she was going to be, so we put her through to the final.

Through what has been explained as a quirk of fate, the four candidates who progressed to that last hustings on the evening of 28 October were all women. Other than Badenoch, those who made their way to the hall of All Saints Church in West Dulwich were Melanie Hampton, Michelle Lowe and Liz Stevenson. 'It wasn't an all-women shortlist,' insists A'Court, who was the moderator.

It just happened to be that four women were the strongest candidates. There was one particularly strong candidate from Wandsworth, Melanie Hampton, who we thought was going to win it. We thought she was the one to beat. And so we had the final round. CCHQ set the format. There was to be no speech, just questions, and that really played to Kemi's strengths. She came alive. There were fifty or sixty members there and she came into her own. At one point she was asked an obscure question about trains and she spoke for about five minutes in quite some detail. I was astonished. I think we all were. She obviously has a retentive mind and had read up assiduously on a range of issues and she showed she can stand up and talk without much effort. It was an oddball question, but she answered it fluently.

The winner needed at least 50 per cent of the votes. After the first round of voting, Badenoch was ahead of her rivals but had not -

achieved enough support, so it went to a second ballot, at which point she came out the victor and was selected. 'When you sit there on the platform you have no idea how the members are going to vote, but she got it,' says A'Court. 'I brought her back into the hall and she made a short speech of thanks. She's not one to go OTT. She takes things in her stride. But she was obviously pleased. Afterwards we went to the pub.' He adds that John Maples was one of the first to offer his congratulations. 'John wrote to me afterwards to thank me and I remember thinking, "You don't need to thank me; I haven't done anything. She won it through an open process. She won it because she outperformed everyone else." There was no fix or stitch-up for her.'

Some prospective parliamentary candidates have to devote years to finding a seat, but Badenoch had done so at the first time of asking. While her natural ability to think and communicate clearly had ensured she crossed the finish line before her rivals, she could count herself fortunate as well. She was only twenty-eight and she had no formal political experience to speak of, yet she had already earned the right to stand in a national election. What's more, there was a positive mood flowing through the Conservative Party at the time, both in London, where Boris Johnson had recently been voted in as its first ever Tory mayor, and around the country. Tony Blair was long gone from Downing Street; his appointed successor, Gordon Brown, was widely regarded as lacking in some of the essential ingredients required by an election-winning leader; and the global economic crisis was just one factor in the developing narrative that after eleven years in government Labour was a spent force and it was time for a change. While it seems unlikely that anybody in the constituency ever thought Badenoch had a serious chance of becoming an MP at the next election barring some freak occurrence, some in the Dulwich and West Norwood Conservative Association did believe that the conditions were more promising than they had been for twenty years. Moreover, Badenoch had a very valuable eighteen months ahead of her in which to cultivate both the constituency and her own profile, which she did by assiduously attending as many events as she could, including one in Parliament at which she briefly met and was photographed with her political heroine, Margaret Thatcher.

The electoral challenge she faced was to dislodge the sitting Labour MP, Tessa Jowell, a Cabinet minister in the governments of both Blair and, since 2007, Brown. Jowell had held the Dulwich seat since 1992, before the Boundary Commission renamed it Dulwich and West Norwood, and her majority of 8,807 was proof of the fact that she had a strong personal following. This made her a formidable opponent for a political novice like Badenoch. In fact, Dulwich had been a Conservative constituency until Jowell's first victory. The Tories had come second in the two subsequent elections, but in 2005 they had been pushed back into third place by a resurgent Liberal Democrat party. Hopes of improving on the 2005 result were high and Badenoch threw herself into the effort quickly. One of her first official engagements was the Southwark Pensioners' Parliament debate, held in February 2009 at Portcullis House in Westminster alongside two senior London MPs, Harriet Harman of the Labour Party and Simon Hughes of the Liberal Democrats. Badenoch was invited along as the Conservatives' representative at only forty-eight hours' notice despite the event having been planned months in advance, but she wanted to make an impact and she is said to have performed well.

She used her connections and her energy to try to drum up support in whatever way she could. One early backer was Graham

Brady, who had been an MP since 1997. 'I first met Kemi after I'd resigned from the shadow front bench over the issue of grammar schools, which I supported but which David Willetts, who was then the shadow Education Secretary, did not,' he says.

> I was invited to speak at a fundraising event in Dulwich and West Norwood. Part of my speech was a defence of grammar schools. Kemi was asked to do the vote of thanks. I had expected her – for perfectly understandable reasons – not to touch on the topic of grammar schools. But instead of swerving this rather contentious issue, she confronted it and told everybody gathered that she agreed with me. Even at that early stage in her career, she did not shy away from the fight.

Another sitting MP to receive a call was Ed Vaizey, by then a shadow arts minister, whom Badenoch had met through the Globalisation and Global Poverty Policy Group. He visited the area to help lobby for extra funds for South Norwood Library. A third MP to endorse her was Peter Lilley. 'Kemi asked me to go and speak at her association once she'd been selected, which I did,' Lilley confirms. 'I remember she also had a rather good fundraising event with Lord Wolfson. Somehow she got him to come and give a speech for her campaign.' Her distant cousin Feyi Fawehinmi was present at that event. 'I realised she was serious about politics when she held the fundraiser with Lord Wolfson, the CEO of Next,' he says.

> Lord Wolfson was so enthusiastic about her. At the time I thought Kemi was just another person who worked in the City who was interested in politics on the side. We used to chat at the time, but then she raised a few thousand pounds or more and I thought,

'If you have a day job in a bank and by night you can get Simon Wolfson to come to your fundraiser, I'm impressed.' It was a chance to meet people from another side of Kemi's life. It was quite an eye-opener for me.

All the while, she did her best to keep her name in the spotlight, sometimes by challenging what she saw as the lazy pigeonholing of black people by those on the left. For example, in September 2009, Baroness Scotland, the first woman and the first ethnic minority person to become Attorney General, was fined £5,000 after she was exposed by the *Daily Mail* for employing an illegal immigrant as her housekeeper. The Conservatives lobbied hard for Scotland's immediate resignation, yet Gordon Brown refused to buckle. When Tessa Jowell was asked about the scandal, she too backed Scotland. One of the arguments Jowell deployed in her colleague's defence was that 'what [Scotland] represented for young black women has been amazing'. Badenoch was outraged and wrote to the *Evening Standard* to take issue with her remarks.

I find it unbelievable that my opponent, Tessa Jowell, has praised Baroness Scotland as 'outstanding', and a role model for young black women. As a 29-year-old black woman, I can state categorically that Baroness Scotland is no role model of mine. The Attorney General has broken a law that she herself drove through parliament. It is inappropriate and patronising to brush off law-breaking on the basis of someone's ethnicity. For Ms Jowell to claim her as a role model on behalf of young black women is typical of New Labour's smug and patronising manner towards ethnic minorities. It is as ridiculous and grating as me claiming Ms Jowell is 'a role model for old white women.'

The letter was not published in full by the newspaper, but excerpts of it did find their way into the *Standard*'s diary column. It is hard to escape the conclusion that Badenoch felt so cross about Jowell's apparently patronising attitude that she would have written this whether Jowell had been her opponent or not, for two months later she wrote to the *Standard* again. This time, her ire was caused by an article by the actor and playwright Kwame Kwei-Armah, who was promoting his play *Seize the Day*, which uses a black candidate's attempt to become the Mayor of London to explore themes of racism and classism. Countering Kwei-Armah's black versus white stance, Badenoch declared Britain to be 'the least racist country on earth'.

It wasn't just Labour politicians and left-wing playwrights who were in her sights, though. The right-of-centre press also incurred her displeasure. In February 2010, the *Mail on Sunday* published a news story headlined 'Revealed: David Cameron's "Obama Army", ready to change the face of the Conservative Party'. The article began: 'These are the 44 black, Asian and ethnic minority Tory candidates in the front line of David Cameron's Election crusade to change the face of the Conservative Party for ever.' Badenoch had by this time set up a personal website on which she would sometimes share her opinions. 'People seem more interested in my being young/black/female than on my political views and I'm often misquoted or misrepresented, so I correct any mistakes here,' she wrote. In response to the *Mail on Sunday*'s political reporting, she shot back: 'More ethnic minority stereo-typing as they call us "The Obama Army". The way it's written almost implies that ethnic minorities can't get ahead without a leg-up.' Soon afterwards, its sister title, the *Daily Mail*, was also given a public tickling off. Badenoch was among a group of thirteen Conservative candidates who had agreed to be photographed on the eve of the general election being called. They were described as

David Cameron's 'new fighting force; the secret weapon with which he believes he will win the war' and given the rather nauseating nickname 'Dave's Dolls'. Among them were future Cabinet ministers Priti Patel and Penny Mordaunt and future minister Helen Grant. In the piece, Badenoch was said to have been selected 'from [an] all female shortlist – though party members claim it was based on merit alone'. To this, Badenoch wrote on her website: 'I WAS NOT SELECTED FROM AN ALL FEMALE SHORTLIST. It is especially frustrating because I am opposed to these types of shortlists that exclude people because of their race, gender etc, yet many people will believe after reading this that I benefited from a fixed list.'

Perhaps surprisingly, the one national newspaper with which she had no cause for complaint was *The Guardian*. She wrote a first-person piece for the left-wing publication that required no photo shoot and no fuss. Instead, she was simply allowed to set out her position in print. In the article, she explained that at the various public meetings she organised in churches and pubs around the Dulwich and West Norwood constituency, the one question she was guaranteed to be asked was 'Why does a young black woman want to be a Conservative MP?' Badenoch wrote: 'The questioner usually seems puzzled when I say I'm an economic liberal who believes in a small, fiscally prudent state.'

Along with five other female Tory candidates, she also gave an interview to the journalist Janice Turner before the 2010 election which is worth recounting for the evidence of Badenoch's political instincts that it provided. In a piece for *The Times* published in February 2024, Turner recalled this interview as follows:

I asked who would call herself a feminist and Kemi was one of only two who raised a hand. To the question, 'What was the last issue that made you shout at the TV?' replies ranged from unaffordable childcare to NHS red tape. But Kemi, then thirty, replied, 'I hate identity politics.'

As she looked back on their initial encounter fourteen years previously, Turner concluded: 'Long before the phrase was common parlance, let alone dominated political discourse, Badenoch's views were fully formed.'

Appearances in the press were all very well, but they would not, ultimately, determine her political future. The real work had to be done in the constituency she was trying to win. It was urban and diverse, taking in parts of Brixton in the north as well as Herne Hill, Dulwich and, in its southern reaches, West Norwood. With a large African and Caribbean population that was naturally inclined to vote Labour, and with about a third of its residents living in social housing, her mission must have felt daunting at times. By the turn of 2010, a strategy had been devised for the so-called long campaign and the local party members were primed to begin the onerous duty of leafleting.

In this, they were helped by a young man who had joined the association in 2008, Hamish Badenoch, a Cambridge University-educated banker. His teenage years had been spent at Ampleforth, the North Yorkshire boarding school then run by Benedictine monks, where he rose to become Head Monitor. In a varied professional career, he had been a journalist in Malawi, a management consultant in Nigeria and run an Avis car hire franchise in Kenya before returning to London, where he worked for the corporate arm of Barclays Bank and, later, Deutsche Bank. He had always been regarded by friends as responsible and steady and it soon became obvious that he also harboured national political ambitions. He and

Kemi quickly struck up a friendship after realising they had been born in the same hospital, St Teresa's, a year apart. 'Kemi thought Hamish gallant when, during one Conservative Party conference which they attended early in their friendship, he remonstrated with the *Mail on Sunday* columnist Peter Hitchens after he was apparently rude about her,' says a friend. A former association member adds:

> Hamish lived very near Kemi in Herne Hill and because he had a car and Kemi didn't, he volunteered to pick her up and drop her back when we had meetings. You could see what was happening. You could tell that there was a relationship developing. It was a nice thing. They got together in the run-up to the campaign and were an item by the time the campaign began.

It was decided that he would also be her campaign manager.

On 6 April 2010, Gordon Brown sought the Queen's permission to dissolve Parliament the following week ahead of a general election on 6 May, marking the start of the short campaign. Badenoch drew up six issues that she considered to be the most important to voters in the constituency: young people, education, businesses, crime, transport and old people. Russell A'Court has mixed memories of Badenoch's general approach to campaigning. 'She had very strong views on what she wanted to do,' he says.

> There was some friction because there were people on the team who'd been campaigning a long time and she didn't always listen to their advice. I remember having a bit of a frustrating conversation with her because she wanted to do a newsletter in a very Labour area of the constituency. When you're fighting an election, you focus on areas where you've got the maximum amount

of support. Also, the issues she wanted to run with didn't always resonate. I remember saying to her, 'Kemi… we have been doing this quite a long time and getting good results.' We'd punched above our weight in local government for a while. We had a long conversation about it over the phone. I was seeking to correct and change a few things which weren't right.

On the other hand, A'Court was always struck by her public speaking ability – a skill that not every politician possesses. 'She was very good in public meetings,' he says. 'You could put her on any platform in any part of the constituency and you always felt confident that she would acquit herself well.'

Timekeeping was not, apparently, one of Badenoch's fortes. 'We used to have a campaign meeting every Saturday morning without fail at nine o'clock,' says A'Court.

And by 9.01 the meeting would have begun and everyone was setting out their plans and raising their issues. The meeting would close promptly at 9.44 and we'd be out the door at 9.45. And just as we were leaving Kemi would turn up and say, 'You're going?' and we'd say, 'Yes, the meeting was at nine.' That became a bit of a feature. Our meetings were always tightly scheduled, and I think that irritated her. That was her quirk and we used to joke about it.

Andrew Gibson, who was a Tory councillor in the Gipsy Hill ward at the time, agrees. 'I voted for Kemi to be our prospective parliamentary candidate in 2008 and had quite extensive dealings with her during the campaign,' he says.

I'm a Thatcherite and I was impressed by her. She was on the centre-right of the party and she was intelligent and articulate. But my experience of her was very negative. We'd have big campaign meetings on Saturday mornings and there'd be representatives from each ward team. And everyone was very supportive of Kemi. Sadly, she was prone to turning up late, complaining and picking fights with some of the other members of the association.

When asked if he ever reproached her, he added, 'She has this sort of "Don't question me" glare. She's volatile. So when she turned up late, she wouldn't apologise, she would glare.'

Based on Gibson's account, it is clear that there were other tensions, one of which related to the fact that the general election would take place on the same day as the local elections across the thirty-two London boroughs. There were eight wards in total in Dulwich and West Norwood. In the south of the borough, the Tories had twelve councillors and controlled four wards. 'We had a chance of winning the councillorships but almost no chance of returning an MP,' says Gibson.

We were always civil to each other, but she's an ingrate. We had our campaigns to run, but she had no empathy for the fact that we were serious candidates for the council. What's more, she was piggybacking on our efforts. We had well-designed newsletters going out and excellent delivery networks which had been built up over years. We put her on the front page of our literature. So Kemi piggybacked onto our campaigns. We'd put her name to various local campaign issues as though she'd been part of things. But for the four teams of councillors that had always functioned well, she could be a difficult colleague. In my opinion, she sometimes treated people like servants.

A further sore point concerned what Gibson and apparently others perceived as a conflict of interest involving Hamish Badenoch.

> Hamish wasn't particularly helpful because he was deputy chairman with responsibility for campaigns within the association and he was standing to be a councillor in the Herne Hill ward. To be blunt, it was a no-hoper. People with experience told him he wouldn't win there, but Hamish put a lot of resources into it and it was a complete waste of time. He came fourth. Some of us were a bit annoyed with Hamish because we weren't aware that he and Kemi were in a relationship and the resources which were going into Herne Hill were justified by him on the grounds that 'it's still worth it because we have a parliamentary election as well'.

Gibson freely admits that he is torn when it comes to Kemi Badenoch's political future. 'Kemi was viewed by some of us as a burden and not as an asset,' he says. 'She and I agree on a lot politically and she is sincere in her views. She does have fully formulated views. But I don't know if I could vote for her in a future leadership election.'

On the campaign trail in 2010, she was invited to take part in local radio debates with the Labour candidate in the neighbouring constituency of Streatham, Chuka Umunna. They had several things in common, being similar in age and both seeking a seat for the first time. Some African media outlets showed interest because they were also both of Nigerian heritage, as was another Labour candidate, Chi Onwurah, who was contesting the constituency of Newcastle upon Tyne Central. Tosin Sulaiman, a journalist for a Nigerian website called NEXT, spent a morning with Badenoch that spring in order to write a profile of her. During their encounter, Badenoch commented on her chances compared with those of Umunna and Onwurah: 'I have a much harder task because I'm trying to get rid of a Labour MP. They're not fighting a campaign. They're just doing publicity. I'm actually fighting.' When she and the journalist visited an area of Brixton in which a lot of Nigerians lived in council accommodation, she was prepared to expand on this statement, explaining that most Nigerian immigrants voted Labour because it was seen as the party that was most friendly to them. 'Many of them may not have come into the country legally,' she said.

> [They believe] Labour regularised them. It's just fascinating. They don't care about their standard of living or what the schools are offering their kids. It's just 'my immigration papers'. This is the toughest place for us. The Nigerians who live in other areas are a lot more amenable because they're wealthier.

There followed a description of a scene in which, ironically, Badenoch was seen to potentially convert one Nigerian voter. He was said to be 'a short, plump middle aged man' known as Uncle Sonny. When Badenoch knocked on his council flat door, she introduced herself and, speaking a hybrid of Yoruba and English, he reportedly said, 'Consa? No way. Never. Never. Ko possible. E ba ti lo si party to favour foreigners. For ten years, I suffered under Margaret Thatcher. I suffered a lot.' Badenoch herself then partly slipped into the same language as she countered: 'I'm working so hard. I don't want Naijas to have no part in it. If I win without Naijas, it's not good. Conservatives are most likely to win. They don't need me to win but if they win, won't it be good if I'm there rather than have no Naijas there?' Uncle Sonny apparently came round to her way of thinking, not only agreeing to vote for her and display one of her posters but even taking two extra posters to give to his friends.

As the campaign reached its closing stages, Badenoch drafted in whatever help she could muster. Her distant cousin Feyi Fawehinmi was among the volunteers and, like Uncle Sonny, he soon came round to the Tory candidate's way of thinking. 'When I arrived in Britain, I voted for Tony Blair the first time I voted,' he says.

It was almost by default. There's an assumption new arrivals in Britain will vote for Labour. Kemi really challenged my views. She made me see we were not that far apart on many things. And she introduced me to Thomas Sowell by giving me one of his books. Anybody who has read his work will tell you once you've read the first one you're hungry for more of his stuff. He really expands your mind in a certain way. What really changed my mind was when I was campaigning with Kemi and I hung out with Tories. Before then, I thought they were a species who you don't go near because they are weird or racist. The first time I went leafleting for her I went down there on a Saturday morning. I was the only black guy. Everyone else was white other than Kemi. I spent hours with them and I realised they were just normal people. It sounds crazy now but at the time it was a shock. Kemi was my gateway drug. I'm a party member now.

Sometimes Badenoch's brother, Folahan, would accompany her on the doorstep despite also having voted Labour previously. And their father, Femi, flew in from Lagos for the campaign and took up a notably active role on behalf of his eldest daughter. 'I would regularly go to Brixton after work or at weekends or to help her leaflet,' her brother recalls.

It was always a long shot as it was a Labour safe seat. Our late father was so proud and excited that he spent the six weeks lead-ing up to the election at her side. He even got the names of local Nigerians and their addresses from the council and we went knocking on doors together. He had thought that a bit of a per-sonal touch from a fellow indigenous Nigerian would win their votes. On the contrary, rather than pledging their votes, many expressed concern and disappointment that he could allow his daughter to be a Conservative.

It was indeed heavy going at times, to say nothing of dispiriting. Fawehinmi adds:

Some people would see we were campaigning for a Tory and tell us to get lost. It was pretty much all negative. I think one person said, 'I'm going to vote for her based on what you've said.' Another said, 'We like the message, we like her boldness and her courage in taking on a former Cabinet minister, but we vote Labour here.'

Looking back on the campaign a year later, Badenoch told a TED Talk audience that those of an African or Caribbean background were not the only ones who were bemused by her party affiliation.

I knocked on this woman's door and I told her what I was doing [and said], 'I'm your Conservative candidate, have you decided how you're going to vote?' And she just looked at me like I was the craziest person and she said, 'You really think that you could defeat Tessa Jowell?' and I said, 'Yes, I wouldn't try if I didn't, you never know what's going to happen.' And she said, 'After everything that we've done for you people, you think that the best thing to do is campaign against Labour?' And I'd just never heard anything like that before. And she looked at me [as if to say], 'How dare you dream so far?'

By the time the count started at Lambeth Town Hall on the night of 6 May, it was obvious to Badenoch's team that there would be no electoral miracle. The question for her was whether she had done enough to improve the Tories' position by coming second. As it turned out, she had not. Tessa Jowell topped the poll with 22,461 votes. The Liberal Democrat candidate, Jonathan Mitchell, came second with 13,096 votes – an increase of almost 3,000 on the previous election. Badenoch finished third with 10,684 votes. She could feel pleased that she had nudged the Tory vote up by almost 1,500 since 2005, and that she had marginally increased the share of the vote by 1.3 points, but there was little else to celebrate, not least because only eight of the Tories' twelve councillors were re-elected.

'The night before the election I was leafleting in Brixton with Hamish,' recalls Fawehinmi.

I was depressed. The Tories were doing well in the polls when we had started campaigning, so it was possible that she could come a strong second. I sensed that she was disappointed [when she realised she might not] but she has that thing which is necessary in politics, which is to put a loss behind you quickly and move on. She was the one cheering us up. It did hit her hard, but it didn't last long.

Her brother adds:

Three years after that election, Margaret Thatcher died, and I recall seeing party scenes from Brixton on the news, and in that moment I knew it was an impossible seat to win. Kemi would have known that too, but she campaigned really well and left an impression on many people, which she capitalised on as she became even more committed to and active within the party after the David Cameron victory.

The Conservatives had indeed managed to secure the most votes nationally and, with 306 seats in Parliament, the largest number of MPs, but they fell short of achieving an overall majority. After five days of talks, it was agreed that they would enter into a coalition government with the Liberal Democrats in which Cameron would be Prime Minister. Badenoch may not have become an MP that time around, but her participation in the election campaign had been grist to her mill. She had notched up some valuable experience, she had been launched politically and she was now known well both locally and within the wider party. She had also prospered personally thanks to her blossoming relationship with her future husband. For all of these reasons, her link to Dulwich and West Norwood had proved to be a turning point in her life. And she remained determined to win elected office.

CHAPTER 6

EYE OF THE TIGER

Kemi Badenoch may have emerged from her first general election campaign nursing one or two bruises, but she was determined to get back into the saddle as soon as possible. Having concluded that maintaining a link to the Dulwich and West Norwood Conservative Association might be in her interests, she thought she had spied a decent opportunity when the position of association president became vacant and threw her hat into the ring. Some remain perplexed by her decision to do so, however. Given the relatively small size of the association, the role of president is essentially a ceremonial one and it had been understood that David Bradbury, a civil servant and former Southwark councillor, would inherit it. Yet Badenoch stood against him. 'It was almost unheard of,' says one former member. 'She was entitled to do it, of course, but she was roundly defeated. And so she went from being a reasonably popular former parliamentary candidate to losing an election that should never have been held. She completely misjudged the mood.'

As the coalition government grappled with the difficult choices that faced the country, she remained active on the Tory candidates' circuit, but her next formal political outing did not come until May

2012, when the London Assembly elections were held. This 25-member body, whose job as part of the Greater London Authority is to hold the Mayor of London to account, is elected by a form of proportional representation. Fourteen members are directly elected via constituencies. The other eleven members are allocated by a London-wide top-up vote. Badenoch secured a spot for herself on the top-up list. Although Boris Johnson regained the mayoralty that month, the Conservatives did not perform as successfully, winning only three seats via the top-up list. Notably, the Tory candidate from the list who came fourth was a young barrister called Sue-Ellen Fernandes, now better known as Suella Braverman. Badenoch, who knew Fernandes passingly at the time, finished fifth. This result would of course have been disappointing, but, apart from being another electoral experience from which she could learn, the fact that she had stood again demonstrated her commitment to the party. Added to this, her mind was focused on her personal life. She and Hamish were by this time engaged. They were married that September at Farm Street, the Catholic church in Mayfair which is well known as a venue for society weddings. They also had a traditional Nigerian wedding in Lagos.

As already noted, Badenoch is not a religion person and there is a story that helps to explain why not. God was present in her early life through her grandfather, a Methodist minister, though by all accounts her immediate family was no more devout than any other when she was growing up. When she was in her late twenties, her faith was broken by the gruesome case of Josef Fritzl, the Austrian who imprisoned his daughter underground for twenty-four years, raped her thousands of times and fathered seven children with her. He was caught in 2008. 'Kemi told me the Fritzl case had a profound effect on her because it removed one of the foundations of the faith in which she had been raised,' says Alex Burghart, a Conservative colleague.

> That foundation was that God does not test you beyond your endurance. She read about the poor woman who'd been locked in a cellar by her father and how she prayed every day that she'd be rescued. Kemi thought about all the prayers she herself had said, often for trivial and silly things. She told me how she'd have given up every single one of those for the victim not to have experienced the horror that she did. She told me that at that moment she thought to herself, 'There is no God. If there was, he would have answered her prayers before answering mine.' I remember she said to me, 'Something in my mind just switched. It was like a candle going out. I will always have respect for faith, because I understand it, and I understand what it means in people's lives. It's important and for many people it's the only way they cope with life. I respect faith, but I do not believe in God any more. I am now just a cultural Christian rather than a believer in a higher power.'

Within a few months of the wedding, Badenoch was pregnant, but she has said that she was extremely fortunate not to lose the baby. In a 2019 interview with the *Daily Mail*, she recalled that when she went for a regular check-up at twenty weeks, 'a student doctor examined me, frowned and said, "I'll be right back." I thought, "OK, something is wrong." They came back and said, "It looks like you're going into labour." They could see the cervix opening.' Premature babies born before twenty-six weeks run a higher risk of abnormal development, a fact which caused appalling panic to the Badenochs. After waiting twenty-four hours to ensure there was no infection,

Badenoch received the appropriate treatment and was given the all-clear. 'It was absolutely terrifying,' she said. 'It made my husband ill. His mum took care of both of us.' Their daughter, Eniola, was born safely at the normal forty weeks in the summer of 2013.

Soon afterwards, the family left Brixton and moved to Wimbledon, buying a 1930s terraced house for £675,000. By the standards of the London property market, this was a relatively modest purchase for two professionals, particularly given that Hamish had by this point spent more than five years working in investment banking. Offering a clue as to why they may have chosen not to overextend themselves, Badenoch once said that she is plagued by concerns that she and her husband might one day run into financial difficulties. 'My greatest fear, for us personally, is that either Hamish or I will lose our jobs, which is why we are so financially frugal,' she told *The Independent* in 2017. It seems entirely plausible that experiencing Nigeria's economic volatility in the 1980s and 1990s at first hand, and watching the dire effect it had on her father's business, left a scar on her which may never fully disappear. It may also explain why she did not become a full-time mother after her first child was born, remaining an employee of Coutts until the spring of 2015.

Aside from their daughter, the couple's primary focus was politics. In May 2014, Hamish was elected to sit as a Conservative councillor in the London borough of Merton, representing the Village ward, yet he and his wife were both still searching for a seat in Parliament. In a sense, they were in competition with one another. They are said to have had an understanding that if one of them made it to the House of Commons before the other, the partner who was not an MP would continue with their professional career. Friends are very clear that theirs is a partnership built on the assumption that one of them would achieve national elected office sooner or later.

In November 2014, Kemi Badenoch was shortlisted as a candidate for the constituency of Banbury in north Oxfordshire following the announcement that the sitting MP, Sir Tony Baldry, was retiring. The seat having been held by the Conservatives for more than ninety years, it was almost certain that Baldry's successor would be returned to the Commons at the next election. Although Badenoch made it as far as the selection meeting, which took place in front of about 100 members of the North Oxfordshire Conservative Association on the morning of Saturday 8 November, she was unsuccessful. As had been the case in Dulwich and West Norwood six years previously, she was one of four women to be interviewed – the other three being Victoria Prentis, Rachel Joyce and Helen Whately – though again this was coincidental rather than deliberate. There was no all-women shortlist, but in any case Badenoch's sex seems to have been irrelevant, for somebody told her afterwards that she never stood a chance because she was considered 'too urban', which she took as code for a comment on the colour of her skin. Victoria Prentis, who was selected, would eventually rise to be the Attorney General in Rishi Sunak's government.

Four months later, prospective candidates for the constituency of Eddisbury in Cheshire were invited to write to the candidates department to express their interest in being selected to take over from the incumbent, Stephen O'Brien, who had announced that he was vacating after fifteen years' service. Those putting themselves forward had to submit a 500-word statement on the topic 'Why I would make a good Conservative candidate for you'. Badenoch got down to the final three and just five days before Parliament was dissolved for the general election, she made the trip to Cheshire for the adoption meeting. Eddisbury was another solid Tory seat, O'Brien having defended it in 2010 with a majority of more than 13,000, and once again all the contenders were women. Badenoch's rivals were Janet Clowes, a former nurse who was a member of Cheshire East council, and Antoinette Sandbach, a barrister who was a North Wales regional Member of the Welsh Assembly. Before the meeting, Badenoch told the *Winsford Guardian*:

My varied background has given me a unique perspective, from working in minimum wage jobs to improving failing schools. I'm able to understand the concerns of people in this constituency. I'm very excited about the opportunity to bring my skills and experience to benefit residents in Eddisbury. I've been fortunate in life and this is an opportunity for me to give back through public service.

Yet, once again, it was not to be. Sandbach was chosen and she held the seat until 2019, when she was deselected by the local party.

Hamish Badenoch had more luck than his wife, insofar as he was nominated to stand in the May 2015 poll. The snag for him was that he had to do so in a seat that he knew was unwinnable. As the election came into view, he was among a cohort of eleven Conservative candidates from England and Scotland to be sent to Northern Ireland, a place that many of the group had never visited before. Northern Ireland has eighteen parliamentary constituencies and for the first time the Tories fielded prospective MPs in all but two of them, the exceptions being North Belfast and Fermanagh and South Tyrone. Among the group was a London-based councillor and lecturer called Claire-Louise Leyland, who contested West Tyrone. Hamish Badenoch contested Foyle, a stronghold of the pro-nationalist SDLP, which covered the city of Londonderry, or Derry, as nationalists call it.

It would have taken a bit of nerve for a well-spoken middle-class man from England to put himself forward for election in this corner of the United Kingdom, where, despite his Catholicism, he would have been considered a complete outsider. He appears to have made the best of it, though. In comments given to the website Northern Ireland World, he explained that he has Irish roots courtesy of his mother, who was born in the Republic of Ireland. 'After my mother emigrated from Ireland she made a home for herself in Wimbledon. That is where I was born and where I live with my wife and baby daughter,' he said, promising, 'If elected I will make my home in Derry.' He added that he had been a Tory member for more than fifteen years and wanted to pursue 'an alternative to the current politics of Northern Ireland' by boosting the area's economy. 'Foyle is a great constituency,' he said.

> But it's failing to realise its potential. Unemployment is too high, eroding living standards and crushing aspiration (especially among the young). Knocking on doors and meeting residents nearly everyone mentions the collapse of manufacturing and lack of jobs in the North West. If elected as your MP I will be a jobs ambassador for Foyle. I will travel from Derry to Dublin, London to Liverpool and Mumbai to Shanghai lobbying governments and corporations to invest in quality jobs in Foyle.

It may have been a brave effort, but, ultimately, it was a wasted one. At the count, he was found to have come seventh out of seven candidates, polling only 132 votes, or 0.4 per cent of the ballot, and losing his deposit in the process. To the surprise of nobody, none of the candidates sent to Northern Ireland by the Conservatives was returned to Parliament. Nationally, the picture was far brighter, however. The Tories had been locked in an unwanted coalition with the Liberal Democrats since 2010, and many predicted that it would be difficult for the party to extract itself from this arrangement. So there was some amazement – and joy – when it transpired that an outright majority of twelve seats had been achieved. David Cameron was now free to chart his own course as Prime Minister, though he would come unstuck a year later because of his promise to hold the Brexit referendum.

Change in the life of Kemi Badenoch soon followed that Tory victory. In June 2015, she left Coutts to take a job as the head of digital operations at *The Spectator*, known to some as the Conservative Party's in-house journal of ideas. Accepting this post meant a cut in salary, but the upside was that it would bring her into the orbit of a range of influential Conservative figures. 'She was the standout candidate because of her background as a manager at Coutts and because she had a computer engineering degree,' remembers one former colleague.

> The editor, Fraser Nelson, was a big fan of the digital possibilities of the magazine, and Andrew Neil, who was in effect the CEO of the magazine, wanted to bring some more structured management to the digital side of things. Neil was a hard taskmaster, but he was pretty happy with Kemi's work, I think.

The Spectator is a small organisation which relies on a tightly run team of journalists. Resources are limited but freedoms of all kinds are plentiful, in contrast to the corporate straitjacket of Coutts. The prospect of a new professional challenge intrigued Badenoch to such a degree that initially she decided to put her own political ambitions to one side to focus on the task in hand. Her goal was to bring the magazine's hitherto sleepy digital offering into line with comparable publications to help maximise exposure and profits. She had no involvement in the editorial side of the business. 'We were really impressed to get a candidate of her calibre,' says Nelson. 'She was miles ahead of anybody else. She was interested in giving up her high-flying career in banking to come closer to the political world – so a tiny company like us ended up with someone who was far more skilled than we had the budget to accommodate.'

All went well, but within three months of arriving, her political career was unexpectedly revived when she was invited to become a Member of the London Assembly (MLA). This opportunity came about thanks to the aforementioned top-up list. A sitting Tory member, Victoria Borwick, had been elected as the MP for Kensington at the 2015 general election, prompting her to resign her seat at City Hall. Under the rules of the top-up list, the next candidate in line to succeed Borwick was Sue-Ellen Fernandes (the future Suella Braverman). Yet she, too, was elected to the House of Commons in 2015, representing Fareham, and so declined to fill the vacancy created by Borwick. This led to Badenoch, as the next in line on the top-up list, being able to take up Borwick's seat, which she did in September 2015. She combined it with her work for the magazine. 'She asked us if she could be an MLA in addition to her role as tech chief and we agreed,' says Fraser Nelson. 'She said it wouldn't be much work. Taking a second job wasn't unusual at *The Spectator* – a lot of people have a second job. Andrew Neil worked for the BBC at the time, James Forsyth had a *Times* column and I wrote for the *Telegraph*.'

The London Assembly position brought with it a basic salary which rose to £56,269 during her tenure, plus a pension. In many ways, this was a perfect political promotion for an aspiring MP who was long on ambition but short on experience. Although she had been appointed to her post rather than elected in her own right in the traditional sense, it was unquestionably a coup for a novice politician who had never before been so much as a local councillor to be overseeing some of the key elements of one of the largest cities in the world. She immediately took her place on the Police and Crime Committee and on the Transport Committee, and it was clear that she took both briefs seriously. One early piece of work with which she was linked that captured the attention of the media concerned the issue of male rape. A study conducted by Badenoch within her first two months as an MLA found that only one in twenty-five victims reported the crime to police. The following month, she called on Boris Johnson to set up three 'drunk tanks' in the capital in time for the Christmas party season, where those who had over-indulged could be taken instead of clogging up Accident and Emergency departments and police cells. More importantly, after the UK's security alert level was upgraded to 'high' following the slaughter in November 2015 of 130 people in Paris at the hands of Islamist terrorists, Badenoch asked Johnson at Mayor's Question Time to consider installing gunfire detectors in shopping centres, museums and stadiums to help police in London. Other issues she tackled before her first election as an MLA in May 2016 included the spiralling costs of policing the Notting Hill Carnival on a bank holiday Monday and a rise in cases of domestic violence.

In that May 2016 election – Badenoch's first ever win at the ballot box in her own right – Labour dominated, winning a total of nine constituency seats and three list seats to give them twelve members out of a possible twenty-five. The Tories won the remaining five constituency seats and added three in the list selection. But the Tory mayoral candidate Zac Goldsmith, who had been selected to stand as Boris Johnson's successor, was comprehensively beaten following a controversial campaign. Goldsmith's operation was branded racist because of the attacks it made on Labour's candidate, Sadiq Khan, who was accused of being an extremist. Badenoch worked on the campaign and subsequently told the *Evening Standard* of her regrets. 'It was a horrible campaign for us,' she told the newspaper. 'I wish I could go back in time and say, "Stop! This will backfire!"' She did make clear, however, that

> the key attack line was not about Islamic terror – it was: 'This is Jeremy Corbyn's man in London'. That was negative and I didn't really believe it. And then [it was] that Sadiq flip-flops – he tells people what they want to hear. One of the examples was the hanging out with Islamists – [the idea was] it didn't matter who they were as long as there were votes in it, not that he was sympathetic [to them].

By May 2016, Badenoch was the deputy leader of the Conservatives in the London Assembly and had added to her duties the vice-chairmanship of the Economy Committee. She had also ceased working at *The Spectator*. 'Having discovered she was pregnant [with her second child, Ralph], she told me she thought it would be unfair to ask us to keep her job open while she was on maternity leave. So she resigned to have her baby,' says Fraser Nelson.

> She would have been within her rights not to have done that. As an employer, I really appreciated it. We're a small company. We'd have struggled to find someone decent to fill her post as stand in digital chief while she was on maternity leave. Media is so fast moving that tech leadership matters and a year is a long time to

lose. But we didn't lose any time at all, thanks to the way she handled it. It was an unusual thing to do. She did it out of loyalty to the magazine and, moreover, out of a sense of decency, I think. I'd say a sense of decency is perhaps her biggest defining characteristic. Along with a weakness for street fighting.

By this point, the national political picture dominated proceedings, specifically because campaigning for the Brexit referendum was underway. Badenoch and her husband had different views about the European Union. She was pro-Brexit, but he was a Remainer – or, as one friend calls him, a 'Cameroon centrist'. They might engage in lively debate periodically and, as Badenoch herself has joked, he even thrust a pro-EU leaflet at her one afternoon outside their local train station, where he was campaigning. But it was never an issue that was likely to cloud their marriage. 'Hamish is half the brains of the operation,' says one friend. 'He is Kemi's chief adviser and acts as a useful counterbalance to some of her views. Anyone who claims she doesn't understand the One Nation wing of the party is reminded that she wakes up beside a Remainer every morning.' On polling day, she described the choice as being between 'the devil and the deep blue sea' but in a mocked-up voting form on Twitter she put an 'X' by the latter, publicly confirming her decision to quit the bloc.

David Cameron resigned just a few hours after it was confirmed that his Remain side had lost the referendum, triggering a Tory leadership contest that was, ultimately, to have profound consequences for Badenoch. It was abandoned when Andrea Leadsom withdrew, leaving Theresa May as the only candidate before party members had an opportunity to vote. May was crowned leader and automatically became Prime Minister on 13 July. Britain's new premier had, like her predecessor, campaigned to stay in the EU, placing her at odds with the majority of voters and with many in her own parliamentary party. Some warned at the time that this did not augur well for Mrs May, and they would be proved right.

While representatives from the UK and EU began to grapple with the complicated process of negotiating Britain's departure from the bloc in the months following May's arrival in Downing Street, political business continued as usual in Britain. Four by-elections took place between December 2016 and February 2017. The Tories lost the first, in the south-west London seat of Richmond Park, which had previously been held by Zac Goldsmith; they comfortably retained the second, at Sleaford and North Hykeham, in Lincolnshire; they failed to capture the third, which was the Labour bastion of Stoke-on-Trent Central; but in the fourth, Copeland, in Cumbria, they caused a shock by overturning Labour's majority with a 6.7-point swing. This marked the first time a governing party had gained a constituency in a by-election since 1982.

Perhaps emboldened by this victory, and well aware that the Labour Party, under its hard-left leader Jeremy Corbyn, was stuck at about 25 per cent in most opinion polls, May took an uncharacteristic gamble in the spring of 2017 by calling a general election. She announced her plan on 18 April, and when a parliamentary vote was held the next day, in keeping with the provisions of the Fixed-Term Parliaments Act, the threshold of two thirds of MPs voting to dissolve Parliament was cleared. This paved the way for the campaign to begin on 3 May ahead of the ballot on 8 June. At that stage, the Tories had a slender working majority of seventeen seats and May told the BBC she hoped to increase her party's tally of MPs in order to 'strengthen the UK's hand' in the Brexit negotiations. She had already made clear her belief that a clean break from Brussels was preferable. In January 2017, she told EU chiefs that she would rather 'no deal' than a 'bad deal for Britain'. Although the 2017 election was billed by some commentators as the Brexit election, however, the reality was quite different.

After May's announcement, there followed something of a scramble within the Conservative Party to fill vacant constituencies before the campaign began and Badenoch was in the thick of it. She had not expected there to be an election until 2019 or 2020 and had even confided in friends that she was unsure if she would ever manage to clear the hurdle of a selection meeting again. At the same time, she was determined to have a go. For this reason, she was not above tapping members of her network to see if they could put in a good word for her. 'As we came close to the election, she had still not been adopted for a seat and she wasn't getting any interviews either,' recalls Sir Graham Brady, who at that point had been the chairman of the backbench 1922 Committee of MPs for seven years. 'She rang me and asked if I could help. I said I'd see what I could do and I contacted CCHQ and explained that she's really good and certainly deserved to be interviewed for a seat.' Who knows whether this worked, but as it turned out, fortune soon came calling – twice.

First, she was shortlisted for Hampstead and Kilburn in north-west London. Originally, three candidates were invited to try out for this Labour-held marginal, but one turned down the opportunity and Badenoch was asked to join the list as a replacement. One of her rivals for the selection meeting held on 25 April was Claire-Louise Leyland, a local councillor in the constituency who had stood with Hamish Badenoch in Northern Ireland two years previously. The other was Henry Newman, who was at that time the director of the Eurosceptic Open Europe think tank, as well as being a local councillor in north London and a former adviser to Michael Gove and

Francis Maude. Leyland won. This rejection, so close to the election, must have been felt keenly by Badenoch, especially because winnable seats in her left-leaning home city were – and are – not taken for granted by the Conservatives. Labour's majority of just 1,138 votes meant that it was a prime target. Yet her failure to win the nomination there turned out to be a blessing in disguise. First of all, it left her available for one of the last remaining Tory seats to become vacant. Secondly, when the results came in at Hampstead and Kilburn six weeks later, Labour held the seat with an increased majority of more than 15,000 votes.

A few hours before the selection meeting at Hampstead and Kilburn began, there was an unforeseen development. Sir Alan Haselhurst, the MP for Saffron Walden since 1977, announced that he was going to stand down. He had attained a majority of almost 25,000 votes in 2015, making this large and diverse Essex seat one of the most pro-Tory in Britain. The adoption meeting to determine who would replace him would be held on 2 May, the night before the general election campaign began in earnest. Whoever left the meeting as his chosen successor would be virtually guaranteed a place in the Commons.

As Badenoch was absorbing the news that she had failed to win in north London, she was told that she had been shortlisted at Saffron Walden, giving her a few days to prepare for the adoption meeting. The other candidates were Laura Farris, a barrister whose late father, Sir Michael McNair-Wilson, and uncle, Sir Patrick McNair-Wilson, had both been Tory MPs; and Stephen Parkinson (now Lord Parkinson) who was at that time Theresa May's political secretary. All three were asked to submit a CV detailing aspects of their personal life and professional career for the benefit of the local membership, which at the time was about 1,000-strong. They then had a few days to prepare for the meeting, which was to be held at Saffron Walden Town Hall. The format was traditional: each candidate would be required to make a short speech before fielding questions for about twenty minutes.

The Badenochs quickly made the journey from Wimbledon to Essex to meet Sir Alan and to familiarise themselves with a constituency that covers more than 400 square miles and is both rural and yet also dependent on one major employer, Stansted Airport. Although Sir Alan personally had been opposed to Brexit, this part of Essex had voted for it in the previous year's referendum, and with that issue running ever hotter around the country, it was of course useful that Badenoch would be able to speak from the heart on this topic. (Hamish, incidentally, had by this point been placed in charge of laying the ground for London-based Deutsche Bank employees to relocate to the EU should the need arise.) She would need to be ready to speak fluently about the national political picture, but, given that the members had not had a chance to select an alternative to Sir Alan for forty years, she could also expect to be grilled on local concerns – not least because campaigning for the local elections was taking place. Saffron Walden's residents comprised London commuters and those who worked at Stansted Airport but also voters with an interest in countryside affairs, including farmers and the pro-hunting lobby. One matter that had troubled the local population around that time was a camp that had been set up by a group of travellers.

On the evening of the contest, the three candidates gathered in a makeshift green room at the town hall. Lots were drawn and it was agreed that Farris would speak first, followed by Parkinson and then Badenoch. The candidates did not know each other well, making it easy to keep small talk to a minimum as they waited to take their turn. Stephen Parkinson recalls, 'Kemi sat quietly listening on her headphones to, I think, "Eye of the Tiger" or "Simply the Best" or some sort of motivational song, which is a technique that various others have used, and that clearly worked and put her in a good spot.' Waiting behind the scenes as your rivals attempt to persuade the members to back them is a form of torture, Parkinson admits. 'You can hear the applause and you wonder, "Oh, was that louder than mine?" But you never really know.'

If Badenoch felt nervous, however, perhaps she need not have done. According to Alex Fuller, who worked as Sir Alan Haselhurst's parliamentary assistant and was present on the night of the contest, Parkinson was placed at an immediate disadvantage compared to Farris and Badenoch. 'To be honest, I think Stephen lost it before he even started,' says Fuller. 'The consensus was that he'd been parachuted in. He was seen as the CCHQ candidate. It didn't make a lot of sense, because Kemi was from Wimbledon [and Parkinson grew up in East Anglia], but that was the sense I got from speaking to people on the night.' Badenoch had two other advantages. She was still fairly fresh from the rigours of the Kilburn contest and would have had time to think about how to improve her performance of the previous week. As the final candidate, she would also potentially be able to leave a lasting impression on the 150-strong audience. 'It's a strange experience,' says Parkinson.

> You have a five-minute speech and about twenty minutes of questions. And on the basis of those twenty-five minutes, the local association decide who they might spend their next twenty-five years with campaigning and so on. So you don't have terribly long to tell your story and make your pitch. And obviously, as the Prime Minister's political secretary, and having been a special adviser before that, trying to overcome the natural scepticism of

a Conservative association about the sort of apparatchik in front of them [is hard].

Parkinson says he told his life story and spoke about his values and his upbringing in East Anglia. 'Stephen gave a very polished speech which was well researched,' remembers Fuller. 'Kemi's speech was more focused on her and her personal journey. She made a great speech and answered questions very directly, which contrasted with the other two candidates.' She was apparently asked about the travellers' site and gave what has been described as 'quite a robust' answer, which went down well.

The local association chairman, Keith Eden, officiated. Once the votes had been cast, the ballot papers were counted in the green room in front of the candidates. 'You could just see the piles going up,' recalls Parkinson.

And it became quite clear that Kemi was ahead. Kemi, I think, prevailed by about a dozen votes. I can't remember the exact figures because a selection meeting is a bit of a blur. And then she was taken through as the victorious candidate and obviously in a snap election like that, straight into the campaign. So it was over quite quickly. But it was a friendly experience. And I was pleased as well to see Laura Farris elected just two years later.

Among the first to offer his congratulations was Fraser Nelson, who published a piece about Badenoch's victory on *The Spectator*'s website that night. 'I suspect that we'll soon be hearing a lot more about, and from, Kemi,' he wrote. 'She is – to put it politely – not a caricature of a Cameron moderniser.' He went on: 'You're unlikely to meet a more staunch Conservative – and someone who loves the

British way of life because she chose it, rather than was born into it.'
He then revealed:

> When the Brexit referendum was on the cards, and *The Spectator*
> didn't declare its position until the end of the campaign, Kemi
> would ask me what I was thinking: surely this is a no-brainer?
> Britain, or the EU – do we really need to mull? She'd often be
> puzzled as to why so many British people had a low opinion of
> Britain: she thought she'd moved to the greatest country in the
> world, and couldn't work out why everyone didn't see it that way.
> And Londoners, she thought, were often the worst offenders.

He listed her enemies as 'divisive identity politics, liberal elites [and]
"short-term virtue-signalling policies which store up problems for
the future"' and concluded that if she were elected, 'Westminster
will certainly be a more interesting place'.

The next morning, Badenoch went to the local constituency
office to meet Alex Fuller, who had been appointed as her campaign
manager, in order to discuss their battle plan. 'The priority as a new
candidate with no experience of the seat was to get her to as many
places as we could, in front of as many people as we could,' Fuller
explains. 'Saffron Walden is a big seat. There are lots of villages there.
I spent every day of the campaign with her, meeting people, door
knocking, at hustings.' Badenoch, who was able to stay at a friend's
house in Thaxted, was not keen on driving, so Fuller was behind
the wheel. She pledged to campaign on aircraft noise at Stansted,
on school places and on the lack of a decent broadband and mobile
signal, among other things. 'The campaign was intense,' Fuller says.

She had a young family who were sometimes in tow, along with

Hamish. It took its toll on all of us. We were all knackered. But she was brilliant. She was great on the doorstep. People liked talking to her. She had a particular style which is quite rare in politics. She answers questions very directly. If she sees something is wrong, she will say it. That's quite engaging.

Yet there were some occasionally difficult moments, he acknowledges.

She is of a different heritage to quite a significant proportion of that constituency. That did come up a few times. Some people said they wanted someone like them to represent them. They were quite unfriendly. It was implicit rather than explicit. They weren't being overtly racist, but it was obvious that's what they were referring to. She didn't really react. She said she was used to it. I remember one occasion in a fairly small village when I was talking to someone on the doorstep and one person didn't really want to engage and they said as they closed the door, 'I think she should just go back to where she came from.' That wasn't said to Kemi – it was said to me.

Despite the electoral inheritance bequeathed to her by Sir Alan Haselhurst, Badenoch apparently took nothing for granted, making the most of the digital campaign tools CCHQ provided, which offered more accurate data than had been available previously. 'A few weeks ago, I had no idea there'd be an election, let alone that I'd be fighting a winnable seat,' she told the *Evening Standard* during the first weekend of the campaign as she promised to campaign 'for every vote'. She then observed presciently, 'I know many people are expecting our party to do well, but the last two years have shown us that polls aren't always right and elections can be very unpredictable!' Sir Alan was also on hand to help, acting as a reassuring presence as she knocked on doors, and, given his popularity in the area, his endorsement was worth its weight in gold. Although on the brink of being eighty at the time, he is said to have been quicker than anybody else when it came to delivering leaflets. Aside from the many other eager local volunteers, there was outside help as well. 'She was obviously well connected,' says Fuller. 'James Cleverly came up. I remember being impressed by how good her connections were before she'd even become an MP. They came for her, not because CCHQ asked them to come.'

The election night was, to nobody's surprise, one of triumph for Badenoch. She increased the share of Conservative votes from Sir Alan Haselhurst's 57.2 per cent in 2015 to a remarkable 61.8 per cent, or 37,629 votes. Her tally was up by almost 5,000 votes on her predecessor's. 'She inherited a massive majority,' says Alex Fuller. 'And she built on that, getting – I think – the highest vote of any member of the Tory Party since 1935. It was a dream seat. It doesn't get much better.' Arguably, her victory demonstrated something of a paradox. Her status as a black woman from London made her, in some people's eyes, the embodiment of that multi-racial city. And yet her right-of-centre attitudes and opinions had not been sufficiently liked by Conservative Party members in London to earn her a nomination as a parliamentary candidate in a winnable seat there, but they had been embraced in the more traditional surroundings of rural Essex. Nor had many people predicted that she would increase Sir Alan Haselhurst's 25,000 majority. From this very promising beginning, the only way was up.

CHAPTER 7

THE MOTHER OF ALL
PARLIAMENTS

Theresa May's plan to beef up her parliamentary majority ended badly. Indeed, it verged on the calamitous. Far from giving herself a hefty mandate and some room to manoeuvre on Brexit negotiations, she painted herself into a corner. Despite winning the highest share of the vote for over three decades, and increasing the number of votes secured in 2015, the number of Tory seats fell from 330 to 317. Labour under Jeremy Corbyn gained thirty seats, taking its total to 262. Having lost her overall majority, May was forced to rely on a confidence and supply arrangement with the Democratic Unionist Party to push any contentious legislation through Parliament.

The 2017 poll has gone down in history as a textbook example of just how uncertain general election results can be, but one effect of it was that those Tory MPs who were voted in for the first time became closer than they might have done had they been returned in greater numbers. 'There were only about thirty of us who arrived in 2017 and, though people naturally went different ways later on, as a group we tried to stick together,' says Lee Rowley, who had been newly elected for North East Derbyshire. 'I think the existing MPs were a bit shell-shocked and demoralised, but those of us who arrived in 2017 were excited. Kemi was always marked out for success; her maiden speech was rightly highly praised and she immediately struck me as someone who had thought about why she had come to Westminster.'

If the outcome ultimately pointed towards the end of May's premiership, Badenoch's career, by contrast, was very much in the ascendancy. Six weeks later, making her maiden speech in Parliament, she again captured wider attention through her oratorical skills. She admitted to feeling 'humility and excitement' and acknowledged the burden of expectation on her shoulders as she informed members that the last MP for Saffron Walden to make a maiden speech had been Rab Butler, in 1929. Butler, she reminded the chamber, had as a Conservative minister introduced the Education Act 1944, which gave every British child a statutory right to free secondary education.

Having saluted the role of the state, she then displayed her right-wing credentials. 'I am often inexplicably confused with a member of the Labour Party – I cannot think why,' she said with barely concealed sarcasm. From some this point might have sounded disingenuous, given Labour's record on ethnic minority representation in the Commons, but it touches on three characteristics that were thought to give Badenoch a special appeal.

First, simply, was that she was black and state-educated, which was – and is – attractive to a party that admires personal initiative and is anxious to bury any trace of racism. Yet at the same time she appeared uninterested in dwelling on her skin colour, or questions of race more generally, unless absolutely necessary. Friends say she is as colour-blind as many white voters like to think they are. Her former colleague Alex Burghart, another Essex MP who was newly elected in 2017, confirms this is no affectation. It is implicit and central to her disposition. 'It is true she is unusual in being a black woman Tory MP,' he says.

> But she very quickly stood out for who she is rather than what she looks like. Her personality is the most distinguishing factor. I never hear her talk about being unusual in being a black female Tory MP. Sometimes I hear about her Nigerian background, but she mucked in with the party such a long time ago, and the way she sees it is we're all Conservatives and all have shared values. That's the uniting force.

This indifference is perhaps partly a function of her age. At thirty-seven when she entered Parliament, she may have felt immune to the views of her fellow party members, whose average age was then fifty-seven.

A second characteristic is that, while being young enough to be fresh and energetic, she was old enough to come across as sensible by more conventional members. Her education predates the era when it became fashionable to regard somebody's sex, heritage or culture as being as important as their opinions and she had made it clear years before that she had little truck with identity politics more generally.

Her third distinctive selling point is a youthful worldliness. To a traditionally nationalist party, her time living abroad renders any international comparison she might make that much more credible. 'To all intents and purposes, I am a first-generation immigrant,' she said in her maiden speech.

I was born in Wimbledon, but I grew up in Nigeria. I chose to make the United Kingdom my home. Growing up in Nigeria I saw real poverty ... Unlike many colleagues born since 1980, I was unlucky enough to live under socialist policies. It is not something I would wish on anyone, and it is just one of the reasons why I am a Conservative. I believe that the state should provide social security, but it must also provide a means for people to lift themselves out of poverty.

She went on to point out in the speech that 'money cannot be printed and redistribution cannot be successful without first creating wealth'. She quoted the philosopher Edmund Burke's view that 'society is a contract between the dead, the living and those yet to be born'. She namechecked the second-generation Jewish Conservative politician Michael Howard, who once spoke of 'the British dream', as she marvelled that Britain is 'a land where a girl from Nigeria can move, aged sixteen, be accepted as British and have the great honour of representing Saffron Walden'. There was a quick history lesson as she explained that the nineteenth-century radical reformer John Bright is often misquoted as saying that the House of Commons is the mother of all Parliaments. 'What he actually said was that this country is the mother of all Parliaments.' And she hit out at those 'who seek to denigrate the traditions of this Parliament, portraying this House as a bastion of privilege and class'. She went on:

It is no coincidence that those who seek to undermine the institutions of this island – Parliament, monarchy, Church and family – also propagate a world view that sees Britain, and the values we hold dear, as a force for bad in the world. Growing up in Nigeria, the view was rather different. The UK was a beacon, a shining light, a promise of a better life.

Her final flourish was to quote someone whose name has been heard rather less frequently in the Commons chamber. 'As Woody Allen said about sex, "If it's not messy, you're not doing it right," she said.

> The same is true of democracy. It is not always predictable; its results are not always elegant; it can throw up results that no one expected – but we adjust. The British Parliament always has adjusted, and that is why it is the oldest in the world: it takes its lead from the British people.

Two influential commentators were particularly moved by her performance. Charles Moore in the *Daily Telegraph* described it as 'outstandingly good', adding:

> She hit all the right notes – freedom, opportunity, private property, national independence, and (the bit which most commonly gets left out) an understanding of how our particular history matters more than any general theory. Just now, there is much complaint that no one in the front ranks of the Conservative Party has any vision of what Toryism is. Listen to this new recruit.

Peter Oborne in the *Daily Mail* was equally dazzled. 'A star is born,' he praised. 'I predict a brilliant future for Kemi Badenoch ... I don't want to jinx her Commons career, but it must be said that the 37 year old delivered one of the most impressive maiden speeches heard in recent years.' He cited her proud evocation of her heroes

Winston Churchill, Margaret Thatcher and Airey Neave, the latter murdered by the Irish National Liberation Army in a car bomb attack in 1979. He admired her line about the vote for Brexit being 'the greatest-ever vote of confidence in the project of the United Kingdom'. And he concluded: 'Kemi Badenoch is quite something. She can set the Tory Party – and British politics – alight.'

Remembering how much attention was paid to Badenoch during her first weeks in Parliament, Rachel Maclean, another Conservative MP who entered the Commons in 2017, believes there is integrity to Badenoch's political ambition.

> She wanted to become an MP because she really cares about the future of the country. People say that in a glib way, but she really means it because for her it's existential. She's come from somewhere that really was difficult. Her maiden speech reflected that. She talked about hope and opportunity and that was the first thing that struck me about her.

The media is always keen to identify 'rising stars' among a new parliamentary intake, and Badenoch's previous employment at *The Spectator* can only have helped her profile among some journalists. It wasn't long before she was summoned for interviews with the *Daily Express* and *Daily Mail*. That summer she also appeared as a panellist on Radio 4's *Any Questions*. She further supplemented the warm reception she had received in Westminster by making some deftly worded attacks on progressive thinking. Wokery, though a word she dislikes, was a favourite target.

In August, she urged the Conservatives to be more confident in challenging the politics of identity and its rhetoric. 'Only this way can we rebuild trust between groups who have been encouraged to focus on their divisions rather than what they have in common,' she wrote in the *Daily Telegraph*.

> Identity politics may claim to defend the rights of individuals, but increasingly it has become a mechanism for undermining the freedom of people to hold and express an opposing view. The truth is that our freedoms are being subtly eroded in an era where emotion and sentiment are prized above reason and rationality. Everyone in public life should judge ideas on the quality of their contents, not the identity of their proponents … Until such common sense becomes the consensus view, let it be we Conservatives who lead the charge.

Once again she articulated a commonly held sentiment and defended the implicit liberalism of Britain's middle class. But if she was happy to chime with those who are prone to lamenting that many important subjects are, seemingly, not allowed to be discussed openly any longer, she was entirely forthright in seeking to banish any trace of racism from the Conservative Party. Whereas the Tories were perceived as having lagged behind the Labour Party in addressing the issue of race, Badenoch's robust stance on 'slips of the tongue' was unmistakeable. On 10 July 2017, the senior Conservative MP Anne Marie Morris used the outmoded phrase 'n***** in the woodpile' during a Eurosceptic meeting in central London in which a future UK financial services deal with Brussels was being discussed. When the remark was reported, Badenoch told the *Daily Telegraph* it was 'an embarrassment to me as a black woman and to the Conservative Party'. She said, 'I was shocked and appalled to hear her comment. No one should use that sort of language, let alone an MP. I spoke to the Chief Whip about it as soon as I heard to express my dismay.' Senior Tories evidently paid attention, because the whip was immediately removed from Morris, with the encouragement of Theresa May, for a period of five months.

In the recent past, such a term, still in common use a few decades ago among older generations, might have been excused or ignored. Morris, who uttered these words in the week of her 60th birthday, may have felt that she was sufficiently senior to have heard it enough times not to realise how offensive it sounds. What is more definite is that in previous years it would not have been the place of a newly elected Conservative MP to voice such vigorous public criticism of a senior parliamentary colleague. But this counts as an early example of Badenoch showing the way to a section of the political class that was sometimes willing to make excuses for thoughtless xenophobia or casual racism. With Badenoch on the Tory benches, those days were gone.

Other attitudes that she felt belonged in the past also presented themselves around this time. She has recalled being advised by two Tory MPs from the 2015 intake – well-meaning or otherwise – not to write articles for national newspapers. The way to promotion, she was assured, was to keep one's head down and be a dutiful constituency MP. The comment pages of the *Daily Telegraph*, it was suggested, were the preserve of Cabinet ministers and grandees. Reflecting on this subsequently on a *Spectator* podcast, Badenoch was withering in her dismissal of such old-fashioned ideas.

I thought to myself, 'Wow. Why would you say such a thing?' I don't know if it's jealousy or people thinking you're getting too big for your boots, but the idea of telling an MP not to say what they think, to me, is for the birds. It's madness. It's what we're here to do.

As if to prove her point, her reputation continued to grow. While recognising that race had been an issue that was capable of embarrassing the Tories, those who wanted a more modern approach had found few suitable flag-carriers, so Badenoch's confident, unassailable assertion of colour-blind credentials was seized upon. Among the 2017 intake of new Tory MPs, at least, she was seen as something of a leader. Another new MP, Julia Lopez, had met her once before, at a training session with Women2Win, which seeks to prepare Conservative women for Parliament.

> When we got to Westminster, straight away she was a person who was talked about. She and Bob Seely were the self-appointed shop stewards of the intake. When it came to the select committee elections, those who had arrived in 2015 and 2017 got together to try and coordinate a bit. I remember Johnny Mercer and Tom Tugendhat were working with those guys to try to coordinate. She stands out and there was a lot of media interest. She has a natural confidence and self-belief – not only does she get the attention, she's comfortable with it.

Badenoch's first elected position as an MP was as a member of the House of Commons Justice Committee, which she sat on between September 2017 and July 2019.

The early prominence which seemed to be hers by right was all the more remarkable for the chaotic situation in which she had to work. Alex Fuller, her Saffron Walden campaign manager, who became her senior communications adviser during her first eighteen months in Parliament, remembers a stressful search for a base in the Palace of Westminster. 'We were working out of other people's offices for quite a while,' he says.

New MPs aren't always given an office straight away. We were working on tables in the Portcullis House café and anywhere else we had to, including in the depths of the Norman Shaw Building, for about six months. We were finally given an office on the upper committee corridor and it was like a shoebox. If you stood in the middle of the room, you could pretty much touch both walls if you stretched your arms out. Trying to get four people in there was impossible. It was a bit like working for a start-up. But through all that Kemi was pretty calm. She was under a lot of pressure to start delivering, to learn how to do the job, to set up an office and build a team. I never got the impression it was getting on top of her. The stress certainly showed sometimes, but it felt like she had a good handle on things.

These unorthodox working arrangements were not made any easier by the fact that, although Badenoch had quit as a Member of the London Assembly, she and her husband had decided not to relocate to her constituency on a full-time basis. Instead, they opted to remain in Wimbledon and rent a house in Essex. On a practical level, there is no doubt that maintaining two properties is both complicated and expensive. On a political level, Badenoch's status as an outsider in Essex irritated some who lived there. One resident of a village called Littlebury submitted a letter to the *Saffron Walden Reporter* within weeks of her election to voice his scepticism about her. 'I would like to add my congratulations to Kemi Badenoch for winning her seat in Parliament,' he wrote. 'It was only right that someone younger was given the chance of fighting for the vacant seat, but let's not forget that when he first won the seat Sir Alan Haselhurst was a very much younger man.' His tone then changed as he went on: 'Apparently, there was "no one local available to fight for the seat" so they had to go outside. One wonders how hard they looked.' He finished by saying, 'Let's face it, and this is no slight against our member of parliament, the reason she was picked is that central office were able to tick two boxes in one – she's a woman and she is black.'

Leaving aside the fact that, rather than being imposed by central office, she was selected by the members of the local association, who were also given the choice of a man and another woman, both of whom were white, perhaps such hostility would not have existed had the family chosen to live in the seat permanently. On the other hand, Badenoch admitted that summer that she did have concerns for her own safety, and, winning an election just a year after the murder of the Labour MP Jo Cox, she may have concluded that the familiarity of London was preferable to relocating to an area that she could not claim to know well. When the *Daily Telegraph* published a survey saying that three quarters of new MPs wanted to improve security at their homes after experiencing intimidation on the campaign trail, she questioned whether the tradition of putting candidates' addresses in the public domain should be halted, telling the newspaper, 'We should change the requirements from a full address to just which constituency you live in. There are children and non-political relatives that at are risk [under the current rules]. I don't think people realise the dangers.' As it happens, the Badenochs have continued to base themselves in London, renting a house in rural north Essex rather than buying one there.

That autumn's Conservative Party conference was held in Manchester in the first week of October. For the previous three months, questions had lingered about whether Theresa May could carry on as Prime Minister, her failure to boost her mandate in the June general election having dented her position so badly. There was talk of her possibly dismissing her Chancellor, Philip Hammond, or her Foreign Secretary, Boris Johnson, in order to enhance her authority. The continuing lack of clarity as to what the eventual Brexit deal would look like added to an overall sense of unpredictability. This, of course, was made worse by Johnson's cavalier optimism and barely disguised intention to unseat the PM.

The annual conference was supposed to be a chance for May to put her troubles behind her and show that while different factions of the party may be squabbling, as they undoubtedly were, she was the only candidate who could make a deal with Brussels around which all of her MPs – from hardline Brexiteers to reluctant, defeated Remainers – could unite. May had never been well known as an inspiring public speaker, but her effort at this set-piece occasion that year could not have gone worse. She was afflicted by a persistent cough and then interrupted by a prankster, later identified as Simon Brodkin, who presented her with a copy of a P45 redundancy notice that had supposedly been signed by Boris Johnson. When the hall rose at the end of the speech to offer sympathetic applause, Johnson, her likeliest challenger, had to be reminded to stand up. Some saw this as pathos compounded by the pretender's gracelessness.

For Kemi Badenoch, however, the day was memorable for all the right reasons. She had been chosen to introduce the embattled leader to the stage. 'I was with Kemi when she was asked to do Theresa May's conference speech warm-up,' remembers Alex Fuller.

It came about fairly late in the day. I think a request came in from CCHQ. You don't turn that kind of opportunity down, so we were furiously writing right up to the last minute. We were in somebody else's hotel room at one point because we couldn't find a

St Teresa's, the private hospital in Wimbledon where Badenoch was born in January 1980. By coincidence, her husband, Hamish, had been born there exactly a year earlier. It has since been demolished.

73 Itire Road in Lagos, where Badenoch lived until she was thirteen. Her father's medical practice occupied the lower floor and the family lived in a three-bedroom flat above. Electricity and water were often scarce.

© Folajimi Emmanuel

81 Springfield Avenue near Wimbledon, where Badenoch moved in 1996. The owner, Dr Abiola Tilley-Gyado, was a close family friend who let her stay there rent-free after her parents decided she should leave Nigeria. She arrived in London with just £100.

Badenoch in 2009, having been selected to fight Dulwich and West Norwood. She is remembered for her abilities as an orator but also for her poor timekeeping.

GIPSY HILL NEWS

Winter 2009   www.dwnconservatives.com

Cllr Andrew Gibson	Cllr Suzanne Poole	Carl Belgrove	Cllr Graham Pycock	Kemi Adegoke
agibson@lambeth.gov.uk	spoole@lambeth.gov.uk	carlbelgrove@gmail.com	pycock1@btinternet.com	kemi.adegoke@gmail.com
07748 736 451	07946 218 965	07900 958 348	020 8761 4218	07896 360 050

Cash Boost for Norwood Park

Norwood Park has won £75,000 in a borough-wide poll for a new water play area near the children's playground, bringing the total amount raised to £225,000.

When we asked residents for their support we knew they would rally round. The old pool had fallen into a state of disrepair, but years of hard work by the Friends of Norwood Park – supported by Carl, Andrew, Suzanne and Kemi – have finally paid off.

Carl says: *"We'll be making sure the architects take on board residents' views. The final design must blend in with the park and reflect the needs of local families."*

Find more information at:
www.yourgipsyhill.com/norwoodpark

Winning for Gipsy Hill...

20mph zone
Suzanne worked with residents concerned about 'rat-running' cars to secure a 20mph zone for Upper Norwood's residential streets. The Council is now consulting residents about the plans.
www.yourgipsyhill.com/20mph

... and a promise of action

Fair deal for leaseholders
More than 3,500 leaseholders were stung for exorbitant charges earlier this year. The Council now admits it made a 'mistake', but we're still fighting to get the mess sorted out.
www.yourgipsyhill.com/leaseholders

Turn over for more...

Fixing Our Broken Economy

Each of these local residents owe £13,000 of public debt because of Gordon Brown's disastrous economic policies

Britain is mired in the longest recession on record, six months after other economies started to recover. In Dulwich and West Norwood, unemployment has increased by almost sixty percent in one year.

"I was shocked to see the figures", says Kemi. *"In our area, there are 33 jobseekers for each vacancy at Job Centre plus and 1 in 5 young people are out of work."*

In 2007, Labour Lambeth promised to open a training centre in Gipsy Hill for unemployed people to learn new skills and find work. Three years later, nothing has happened.

Kemi adds: *"Norwood's Labour MP opened a training centre near the Olympic Park in East London last month, but hasn't mentioned the lack of similar facilities in South London. Why won't she speak up for local residents?"*

Conservative Promises

- Training focused on the young and long-term unemployed.
- Restoring the link between state pensions and average earnings.
- No Stamp Duty for 9 out of 10 first-time buyers.

Badenoch and her father, Femi, in the early 1980s. He encouraged her politically and in 2010 flew to London to help her on the campaign trail in Dulwich and West Norwood.

The Badenochs in 2022. 'Hamish put her career ahead of his own,' says a friend. 'He is her political confidant as well as her husband. If he said to her that he didn't think her being leader would work for the family, she wouldn't do it.'

Pictured in July 2022 with Penny Mordaunt, Rishi Sunak, Liz Truss and Tom Tugendhat during a Tory leadership TV debate. She surprised many by coming fourth and booked herself a seat in the Cabinet in the process.

© Imageplotter/Alamy Stock Photo

The political relationship between Badenoch and Michael Gove has long been a source of suspicion in Tory circles. He was once her mentor, but in 2023 she publicly criticised his affair with a married friend of hers.

© Tayfun Salci/ZUMA Press Wire/Alamy Stock Photo

'They say a prophet is never loved in their own country,' Badenoch told the BBC in 2020. 'Growing up in Nigeria, Margaret Thatcher was inspirational.'

Badenoch was once so close to Suella Braverman that she helped to organise her hen do. After Braverman stood against her in the 2022 leadership contest, relations cooled.
© Chris Radburn/PA Images/ Alamy Stock Photo

Between 2020 and 2021, Badenoch served as Exchequer Secretary to the Treasury. Simultaneously, she was Minister for Equalities, which took up far more of her time.
© Alberto Pezzali/NurPhoto via Getty Images

Badenoch visiting McDonald's UK headquarters in East Finchley, London, in March 2022. As a teenager in the 1990s she worked at the hamburger chain's Wimbledon outlet, which she has said she found fun.
© Jeff Gilbert/ Alamy Stock Photo

printer. But then when we got there she did brilliantly. It was her speech. She wrote it. I was just on hand just to make suggestions.

Fuller was not alone in thinking that Badenoch performed with aplomb. 'There are very few countries in the world where you can go in one generation from immigrant to parliamentarian,' she told the members, adroitly meeting the hall's expectations. 'That is the British dream.' Her words were received almost as rapturously as her maiden speech in the Commons had been. Afterwards, she complimented May's 'perseverance and determination' in pressing on despite her cough, but she also managed an artful spot of self-deprecation. 'It was all my fault,' she told the *Mail on Sunday*. 'I was the last warm-up speech before the Prime Minister came on, and I got very nervous, so I kept drinking all the water. Then Theresa came on with her dry throat and there was none left.'

The sense that Badenoch had been elevated beyond the status normally granted to new backbench MPs was underscored six weeks later when she was among a select group to be invited to a Christmas party hosted by Rupert Murdoch at his penthouse flat overlooking Green Park. She was joined there by fellow Conservative MPs Tom Tugendhat, Dominic Raab and Rishi Sunak, as she rubbed shoulders with the former Rolling Stone Bill Wyman and the artist Grayson Perry. Journalists at the party included *The Sun*'s political editor Tom Newton Dunn, *Spectator* editor Fraser Nelson and *Daily Mail* editor Paul Dacre. It was a fitting way to round off what for her personally had been an enormously successful year.

The following month, her arrival in the Tory hierarchy was further confirmed when she was appointed a vice-chair of the Conservative Party with oversight of candidate selection, a decent promotion for somebody who had been a candidate herself just seven months earlier. This was taken as evidence that she had impressed a Prime Minister who was anxious to overcome the competing forces around her and, with the appointment of nine new vice-chairs (three with ethnic minority backgrounds), to broaden the appeal of what May had claimed in 2002 was regarded by some as 'the nasty party'. Badenoch's advance was seen as having a degree of window-dressing about it, as sources close to party managers suggested she would be helped in the role by the more experienced Brandon Lewis. Even so, it was a statement of intent, and one to which Badenoch added her own stamp when she ended her husband Hamish's political career by removing him from the candidates list. This was done, she explained, to ensure there were no conflicts of interest on her watch. 'As long as I'm doing this role, I asked him if he minded just stepping off because I don't want that to be part of the argument,' she said. At the same time, she couldn't resist a light-hearted remark at the expense of her 'woke' critics. She went on to say she had anticipated claims that she had axed Hamish because, unlike her, he backed Remain in the referendum and was a 'white public schoolboy'.

By March 2018, Badenoch had begun to refer to herself as a 'classical liberal', a political tradition concerned with defending the rights of the individual against the state that dates back to the seventeenth century and whose followers more recently have embraced the monetarist school of economics. Margaret Thatcher and Ronald Reagan are among them. When the Institute for Economic Affairs think tank launched the 'FREER' initiative that spring, to be run by two new Tory MPs, Lee Rowley and Luke Graham, Badenoch was listed as an active member of the group. She published a paper on freedom of expression, issued that May, in which she wrote of her childhood experiences growing up in a country that was not free, in order to remind those in the West how precious such liberties are and how easily they can be lost. It was an early example of her setting out her liberal-conservative political doctrine and was also important in that it helped to establish her professional relationship with Rowley, which would turn out to be of great importance to her.

All of this showed how quickly Badenoch had settled into her new surroundings. Indeed, so relaxed was she that in April 2018, in response to an interview question from the Core Politics website about 'the naughtiest thing you have ever done', she confessed to having hacked into the website of the senior Labour MP Harriet Harman ten years earlier, amending it to favour the Conservatives. Specifically, she did this when Boris Johnson was standing for the London mayoralty for the first time, putting a large 'Vote Johnson' poster on the homepage.

In one respect this was nothing more than a very modern kind of practical joke. Certainly, she regarded it as harmless fun. Yet her admission was curiously unguarded given that such online trickery can lead to criminal charges and there had been little, if any, prospect of her indiscretion ever coming to light by other means. Owning up to this act drew strong criticism from Mustafa Al-Bassam, a computer science PhD researcher at University College London, who reported the incident to the authorities at Action Fraud, the national reporting centre for cybercrime. 'I hope they do take this matter seriously, and apply the law equally to Tory MPs as they do to hacktivists who have gone to jail for less,' Al-Bassam commented on Twitter. Any prosecution was rendered far less likely by Harman quickly making clear that Badenoch had written to her to apologise and that this expression of regret had been accepted. Badenoch later told the *Spectator* podcast:

I did apologise to Harriet, who is a really lovely person. Obviously we disagree about almost everything, but she is what I call an old school Labour MP where it is not personal, whatever the disagreements are. Some of the newer Labour MPs are so visceral and can't understand how anyone can be a Conservative. Harriet is not like that.

More intriguing is how Badenoch managed to effect the hack. In 2022, she told Katy Balls of *The Spectator* that she had clicked on Harman's website and been asked for a username and password. 'Literally, I typed the first thing that came into my head and I got into the back end of it and, as you know, I'm an engineer and I've done computer science. I thought it's too good not to do anything about.' In case anyone believes this was a major breakthrough by a fiendish Moriarty, Harman's password was made available to readers of the Guido Fawkes website that month (username: harriet, password: harman) after a hacker wrote in to explain how he had used 'log-less multiple proxies' to access Harman's site. Harman herself confirmed to Adam Boulton of Sky News a few days later that this was accurate.

What connection this had with Badenoch's incursion is unclear, but one friend is in no doubt that the ramifications of her transgression continue to be felt by Badenoch years after she admitted to it. 'She felt quite stung by the Harman hacking episode,' says this person.

Still to this day about half of the Twitter content you'll see on any issue to do with Kemi is about that episode. She felt that telling that story was a way of showing off her software skills in an amusing way. But the reaction was hostile and that was a big turning point for her as an MP. There were questions about her trustworthiness and morals. I think she felt she had to change her public-facing persona and be quite tough. I certainly think that's one episode that left a mark. She's not someone who shows an enormous amount of reflection anyway, but she's toned down a lot of her personality.

Back on the political front line, she continued to project the type of rhetoric that traditional Tories wanted to hear. Coming from a black MP who was not yet forty years old, her words arguably carried extra potency. In an interview with *Total Politics*, she accused young people of being excessively strait-laced about sexual advances, far more so than had been the case when she was in her teens. At the very least she was articulating a commonly held sense of society's moral cornerstones having been moved. She centred her remarks on the TV show *Friends*, remarking how newer viewers had been squeamish about particular jokes and plotlines. For example, in one episode a character jokes about his cross-dressing father. In another, a character purportedly has a bad attitude towards his ex-wife's lesbianism. Some had claimed that this made the sitcom transphobic or homophobic. At the time of its original broadcast in the 1990s, these things had been watched and enjoyed globally in the manner intended. Badenoch said that the idea of *Friends* being homophobic or transphobic is

a puritanical position, which I think of as conservative. So, you can't really put your finger on what is what these days. *Friends* was the biggest television series of all time. Everybody loved it, it was syndicated all around the world. The idea that in a few years people are talking about it as if it's this horrific series, for me that just doesn't compute. Something has gone wrong somewhere.

As she settled into her vice-chairman's role, the scenery was wobbling badly higher up the party. Theresa May was battling valiantly to unite her troops, but the Eurosceptic 'ultras' and the formerly Remainer rump were hopelessly split. There appeared to be no compromise position that would be acceptable to Brussels that would fix the situation, and time was running out. Britain was due to leave the EU on 29 March 2019. The Europe issue once again looked likely to be the undoing of a Conservative leader.

One possible accommodation, known as the Chequers deal, was engineered. However, two of May's most senior lieutenants, Brexit Secretary David Davis and Foreign Secretary Boris Johnson, resigned in protest, having initially appeared to accept it. In the case of Johnson, few doubted that he had in fact drawn back in order to make a better jump. Having removed his support, ostensibly on a point of principle, he and his leadership bandwagon began to look unstoppable. All that was needed to achieve his dream of reaching 10 Downing Street was the failure of any deal that May might concoct. She fought on, though, and at the end of November 2018, EU leaders met, with European Commission President Jean-Claude Juncker reiterating his sadness at Britain's departure. Apparently trying to be helpful, Juncker told reporters that May's plan was the best deal possible for Britain. For many on her own benches, though, it was not enough. Among them was Dominic Raab, who resigned as Brexit Secretary after a mere four months in the job.

Enough Conservative MPs had written letters to Sir Graham Brady, the chairman of the backbench 1922 Committee, for a vote of no confidence in the Prime Minister to take place. It was held on 12 December. May won it by 200 votes to 117, allowing her to cling on despite more than one third of the parliamentary party having voted against her. Badenoch, incidentally, backed her. By the end of the year, pundits were reaching deep into the lexicon to describe May's plight. She had voted Remain, but a sense of duty propelled her forwards. Her mission looked increasingly doomed, though, and the way forward for the country seemed equally unclear. Some outside the Conservative Party even called for a second referendum and/or the revoking of Article 50, the legislation designed to trigger the UK's departure from the EU, in the hope of buying time. Britain was riven.

Of this fraught period, Badenoch's ally Julia Lopez MP comments:

Brexit became this highly over-intellectualised shenanigans that was fundamentally about overturning a democratic referendum vote. It was as big a threat to democratic faith as I'd seen. The deal Theresa May put together was deceitful. It would have left us with less power than we had when we were in the EU and when the public realised this, there would be a huge democratic backlash in a way that would be damaging to people's faith in our system. That's why I voted against May's deal. Kemi was not one of the ERG people. She was a Brexiteer, but I think she was willing to give the government the benefit of the doubt. Within government the view was 'Get Brexit done, whatever it takes, and address later the major problems of the deal.' But others – me included – thought the backstop made that nigh-on impossible as the UK would be robbed of any leverage in future negotiations. When it came to meaningful votes, therefore, Lee Rowley and I both voted against the May deal on all three occasions. But it's not as though we judged those who came to a different conclusion. These were not easy judgements to make and they were deliberately made more difficult by the running down of the clock and the muddying of the water by the government.

Many who are today regarded as the heroes of the Brexit campaign, including those who eventually swung behind Boris Johnson and his 'Get Brexit Done' slogan, which was used during the general election of December 2019, are less keen now to advertise that for a long time they endorsed the compromises of Theresa May's Chequers deal. This may have been down to an admirable loyalty to their leader, a mistrust of Johnson, or sheer conviction. Only once the deal was doomed did they switch sides. Among them was Kemi Badenoch, who, before May's third (failed) attempt to win over a majority of MPs in the Commons, articulated her support for her leader during a parliamentary debate on the EU (Withdrawal) Act in January 2019. It amounts to what could be described as a model exposition of pragmatism. As such, it is worth quoting at length.

Having stated that she voted for Brexit but entered the Commons a year after the referendum, she said:

> I disagree with some of those on my side who feel that this deal is not what the 17.4 million voted for. I am one of the 17.4 million. I agree with the Prime Minister that no deal is better than a bad deal, but this is not a bad deal. In my maiden speech, I said that democracy was messy. Of course it is. I never expected a perfect deal, and I also knew there would be concessions. Had this deal been on the ballot paper in the 2016 referendum, I would have voted for it as better than remaining.

She justified her support for the deal on the basis that

it gives us full control on services, which are 80 per cent of our economy. I am a free marketeer and, much as I feel we can do well on our own, I like the compromises on state aid and monopoly law – those are good restrictions to prevent our descending into a wholly socialist state. I like the fact that we are leaving the ECJ's jurisdiction and that we are ending free movement.

She added:

People have talked about other options, such as revoking Article 50. That is a terrible idea, one that comes from people who think they can wipe away the referendum and pretend it was all a bad dream. That cannot happen and they should think carefully about the consequences. What would we be saying if we, the UK, the fifth largest economy … cannot leave? If we cannot leave, who can? If we do not leave, why would the EU ever reform? … We need to leave in order to show that it is not a prison but a cooperative organisation and that if it no longer works for people, they can escape it.

She ended by expressing the hope that some of her Conservative colleagues might change their minds. She hoped in vain. In what became known as the 'meaningful vote', MPs rejected May's Brexit deal by 432 against 202 in favour, the largest ever defeat for an incumbent administration. May's government had to face another vote of confidence, held the following day, 16 January 2019. It was won by 325 to 306, a majority of nineteen. A second 'meaningful vote' was defeated in the Commons in early March. Still May insisted that she would carry on, and a week later she asked Donald Tusk, the President of the European Council, for more time. This request was granted, but she was given only until the end of June.

Once again May set about trying to scramble together a Commons majority. As a sop to her opponents, she foreshadowed her own departure, though without specifying a date, only to be defeated again in the Commons on 29 March (286 in favour and 344 against) on a third 'meaningful vote'. Again, May's Eurosceptic rebels would not come into line, to the frustration of some of their younger colleagues. Badenoch told the *Daily Telegraph*, 'We are in a time loop ... people need to move on.' In fact, the only person moving on, after still more blows to her authority in the ensuing weeks, was Theresa May. Just shy of three years after the referendum, Britain was forced to participate in the EU elections on 23 May. The newly established Brexit Party, run by Nigel Farage, trounced the major players, gaining twenty-nine seats. Labour secured ten seats. The Tories sank into fifth place with just four seats. On 24 May, Theresa May resigned, triggering another Tory leadership contest.

The ensuing campaign was what Badenoch called 'probably the most important the party has ever had'. The likeliest winner looked to be Boris Johnson. He promised to 'turbo-charge' negotiations with the EU, threatening to leave without a deal if an acceptable one was not achievable. He had a swagger that some found reckless but few could match. Yet Badenoch decided to resign her vice-chairmanship in order to back the second favourite, Michael Gove, citing his achievements in education and public service reform. According to one friend of Badenoch, she has always got on well with two of Gove's closest allies – his ex-girlfriend turned special adviser Simone Finn and Henry Newman. Writing in *The Sun* on

6 June, Badenoch's target was clear. 'Anyone can make promises,' she opined. 'It is no good just believing in Brexit if you can't actually deliver. I'm suspicious of anyone proposing simple answers – shutting down Parliament until no deal, a snap general election, or an immovable Brexit deadline … If there were simple solutions they would have been tried already.' Having suggested that Johnson was the wrong choice, she explained why she thought Gove was the right choice, comparing him to Margaret Thatcher as she said, 'We have seen before a former education secretary take charge of this country and [lead] it to a brighter future. She won against the odds in 1979, 1983 and 1987.'

That weekend, excerpts of a biography of Gove written by Owen Bennett were published in the *Daily Mail*. These confirmed that Gove had taken cocaine on several occasions while working as a journalist in the 1990s. This revelation went against Gove's comments, also made in the 1990s, condemning those members of the middle classes who wanted to liberalise drug laws. Badenoch introduced him at the formal launch of his leadership bid on 10 June, confirming their closeness, yet the drugs story was undeniably a setback. While the extent of the damage it inflicted on his chances cannot be known, it is a fact that he slipped from second place to third in the final ballot of MPs on 20 June, thereby failing, by two votes, to defeat Jeremy Hunt, who was left to face Boris Johnson in the national party membership run-off. On 23 July, it was announced that Johnson had won the members' vote easily. About 160,000 Conservative Party members were entitled to take part in the final ballot. Johnson achieved 92,153 votes while Jeremy Hunt secured 46,656 votes.

Once in Downing Street, Johnson dismissed more than half of Theresa May's ministers, a move that was said at the time to have represented the most extensive post-war Cabinet reorganisation without a change in the ruling party. The services of Michael Gove, with whom Johnson had had a decidedly uneven relationship in the past, were retained as he was appointed Chancellor of the Duchy of Lancaster. Badenoch had previously expressed admiration for Gove's work in education, so when she was asked to be a parliamentary under-secretary in that department as the Minister for Children and Families, it was known that she had an interest in that brief. Two years after her election as an MP, she had managed to get a foothold on the lowest rung of the ministerial ladder. Her boss was to be Gavin Williamson, the newly appointed Education Secretary. Government briefers suggested that Williamson and Badenoch would complement each other. Badenoch's own status as a former pupil at the state-funded Phoenix College was cited as evidence of her fitness for the job.

At the time of her appointment, though, she was heavily pregnant and due to take six months' maternity leave. Her previous pregnancies had not been straightforward. She had been dogged by sickness – aggravated by the smell of coffee and onions, she said later – for almost their entire duration. She also suffers from high blood pressure, which can create serious problems as the birth approaches, so it was felt particularly important that the baby's arrival, planned for September 2019, should coincide with a quiet period politically.

In the event, the Badenochs' third child, a daughter called Aramide, could scarcely have been born at a stormier time. Somebody less at home in the midst of the political fray than Badenoch might have welcomed a chance to take cover. This meant that she was out of the firing line during this period, leaving her opinions on some highly contentious matters unrecorded. Johnson had announced in

July that Britain would leave the EU on 31 October 2019, whether a Brexit deal had been agreed or not. In late August, UK and EU negotiators agreed to resume regular meetings. Yet Johnson heralded a further political collision by letting it be known that, controversially, he planned to prorogue Parliament for a period of about five weeks, until 14 October. His calculation was that this would reduce the time available for his opponents to block a no-deal Brexit. Johnson's critics believed that he was being spurred on by his chief adviser, Dominic Cummings, and was operating at his most swashbuckling and contentious. The magnitude of his boldness was multiplied by the fact that the Queen's consent was needed. Although the Queen granted it, and Parliament was suspended from 10 September, the Supreme Court overturned the move and MPs returned to Westminster, against Johnson's wishes, from late September.

The Conservatives had not had a parliamentary majority since 2017 and, following the party conferences, it was decided that the only way forward was to call a general election. The six months' maternity leave Badenoch had wanted to take lasted for barely six weeks. On 6 November, Parliament was dissolved ahead of the polls opening on 12 December. Badenoch found herself in the unusual position of campaigning during the short, cold days of November and December in Saffron Walden while pushing her newborn baby in a pram. 'It's not ideal,' she lamented to the *Daily Mail*, admitting that she was 'sleep-deprived and hormonal'. Despite her tiredness, she notched up 39,714 votes in Saffron Walden – an increase of more than 2,000 votes on the previous election – and a remarkable 63 per cent of the total vote. After the customary pleasantries at the count, she thanked the Prime Minister for calling the election. 'We can now break the deadlock that has been in Parliament,' she said.

The message we had at this election was to get Brexit done and that is what I told the constituents I will do and that is what I am going to be doing. I am also a local constituency MP and I have priorities for this area to increase school funding, better health service and to keep our community safe.

In truth, she was planning to resume her maternity leave and go back to Westminster in March 2020. In order to be paid, however, she was required to be sworn in again, and a few days before Christmas, with Aramide strapped to her body in a sling, she presented herself once more to Parliament to take part in this solemn ceremony. Her role in the new government was to be put on hold while she spent time at home. As it turned out, though, her return was to coincide with a new, wholly unanticipated and deadly menace that put the rigours of the Brexit debate in the shade.

CHAPTER 8

EQUALITIES

Kemi Badenoch did not set out to make the colour of her skin central to her political career, but it would not be inaccurate to say that events conspired to make it so. As she has occasionally lamented, in a truly colour-blind world, her views on taxation and personal responsibility – matters on which she feels strongly – would be her preferred subjects for discussion, of no more or less interest than those of any other gifted junior minister. In the real world, however, ambitious politicians have to play the hand they are given. In February 2020, she was appointed to the posts of Exchequer Secretary to the Treasury and Minister for Equalities, increasing her salary to £101,843. But the dry banality of those titles barely hinted at the controversies in which she was to become involved. An early portent came from Pink News, the LGBT website, which pointed out on the day of her appointment to the equalities brief that in the previous year's parliamentary vote on extending same-sex marriage in Northern Ireland, she had abstained. Scrutiny of her beliefs was guaranteed, and so was the sheer relentlessness of the job.

The wider context was the stealthy appearance in the first weeks of the year of a mysterious, highly infectious virus which had originated in China. On 30 January, the World Health Organization declared the outbreak of coronavirus a global public health emergency. By that stage only two people in the UK had tested positive for Covid-19, but Public Health England (PHE) raised the risk level from low to moderate and the government launched a public health campaign, encouraging regular hand-washing. A fortnight later, 1,400 people worldwide had died of (or with) the virus, and by early March the first UK fatalities had been recorded. Amid government reluctance to curtail personal freedoms and an initial scepticism as to its potency, Boris Johnson attended a rugby match at Twickenham on 7 March, shaking hands with others unconcernedly. Yet the government rapidly came to understand its dangers. These were no longer normal times. 'We've all got to be clear; this is the worst public health crisis for a generation,' warned the Prime Minister on television from Downing Street on 12 March. 'I must level with you, level with the British public: many more families are going to lose loved ones before their time.' Eleven days later, a national lockdown was announced, and barely a week after that Johnson himself caught the disease and was later forced to spend three days in the intensive care unit at St Thomas's Hospital in London.

And so began months of fear and uncertainty. How long would the virus last? How was it transmitted? How could economic activity continue? How could the country afford the inevitable downturn and demands for compensation? Could a vaccination be found? Might the virus mutate and become even more dangerous? The government sought to provide reassurance, but it was learning on the job, not always flawlessly. A new mood of national crisis emerged. In Westminster, normal hostilities were paused as politicians struggled to accommodate this spectacular disruption to democracy. By the end of April, the deaths of more than 26,000 Britons had been attributed to coronavirus, but a month later the government, anxious to minimise restrictions on personal freedom, began to bring the lockdown to what would turn out to be a temporary end. The unprecedented disturbance to the economy required emergency surgery from the Treasury. The Chancellor, Rishi Sunak, who had only been appointed in February following the resignation of Sajid Javid, won plaudits for his grasp of the situation and the swiftness and generosity of his response. Kemi Badenoch, as Exchequer Secretary to the Treasury, would have been privy to those calculations, though her name barely featured in newspaper coverage at the time. The soft return to work following the birth of her third child was in fact a very bumpy landing.

In fact, it was subsequent developments unconnected with her Treasury post that pushed her into the headlines. By early June 2020, the British chapter of the campaign organisation Black Lives Matter had begun staging regular protests following the killing in America on 25 May of George Floyd. At the same time, Public Health England published a hastily commissioned report suggesting that people from ethnic minorities were up to twice as likely to die of coronavirus. The Health Secretary, Matt Hancock, said the causes were not fully understood but that people in this category might want to put 'more emphasis' on social distancing and hygiene rules at work to protect themselves. Responding to questions from Labour about racial health inequalities, Hancock said, 'Black lives matter, as do those of the poorest areas of our country which have worse health outcomes, and we need to make sure all of these considerations are taken into account, and action is taken to level-up the health outcomes of people across this country.' He said there was no point in taking specific action to address the issue until it was clear 'how much of it is due to occupation and how much is due to other factors'. To better understand the situation, he asked Badenoch to investigate further in her capacity as the Equalities Minister.

As far as anti-racism campaigners were concerned, Hancock could barely have chosen a more provocative candidate for this task. The SNP MP Alison Thewliss suggested during a Commons debate into the PHE report that the government's 'no recourse to public funds' policy, which prohibits many immigrants from receiving welfare benefits, was part of the problem. 'It is one thing to say "black lives matter" but quite another to force black people and people from BAME backgrounds out to work because they have no choice whether they go to work because they have no recourse to public funds,' Thewliss said. 'No recourse to public funds is a racist policy. Will she abolish it?'

Badenoch replied:

It is wrong to conflate all black people with recent migrants … I'm a black woman who is out at work … It is wrong to conflate different issues and merge them into one just so you can get traction in the press. It's not right for us to use confected outrage. We need courage to say the right things and we need to be courageous to calm down racial tensions, not enflame them just so we have something to put on social media.

It was also pointed out that one placard at a recent Black Lives Matter protest in London had read: 'Being black should not be a death sentence'. Badenoch referred to this as she said:

Let us not in this House use statements like 'being black is a death sentence', which young people out there hear, don't understand the context and continue to believe they live in a society that is against them, when actually this is one of the best countries in the world to be a black person.

This was characteristic of her approach and bound to incense an affronted crowd. Among them was Afua Hirsch, the author of the black history and culture book *Brit(ish): On Race, Identity and Belonging*. Hirsch examined Badenoch's credentials in this area in *The Guardian*. 'On "institutional racism" – a phenomenon that affects minorities in Britain – [Badenoch] has been reported as saying that she doesn't recognise it,' wrote Hirsch.

On former mayoral candidate Zac Goldsmith's Islamophobic campaign? She helped run it. On the black community? She doesn't believe that it really exists. On American racism? 'We don't have all the horrible stuff that's happened in America here,' Badenoch said in 2017. For those of us who see racism for what it is, as a system that kills – both our bodies, and our humanity – this is traumatic. I listened to the Health Secretary, Matt Hancock, announce – as if it was his new discovery – that 'black lives matter', and offer someone as seemingly uninterested in anti-racism as Badenoch as a solution.

Badenoch is rarely one to leave her opponent with the last word and on 7 June she returned to the fray with an article in the *Mail on Sunday*. In it, she said her critics risked inflaming racial tensions – unintentionally, she admitted – and she lambasted the BBC for its website's headline 'Minister rejects systemic racism claims' when the term 'systemic racism' had not even been mentioned in the debate. This was an 'incredibly harmful' claim, she wrote.

By implying that a black Minister has, out of hand, rejected racism as a factor, the hard work done by many ethnic minorities in Government, the NHS and Public Health England is discredited, trust is lost and race relations become worse … Sloppy, agenda-driven journalism of this sort fans the flames of racial division.

She continued with a broadside against much of the media.

We must address prejudice but this is impossible if our national broadcaster, politicians and commentators play a social media game to achieve outrage rather than enlightenment. We must combat the real inequities in society, but we do everyone a disservice if we give in to culture warriors whose relevance depends on inflaming tensions. By hijacking the Government's work to improve the lives of BAME people, those spoiling for a fight are sacrificing the hope of so many young people for little more than clicks, likes and retweets.

In a sense, she managed to be both emollient and antagonistic, applauding those in government and elsewhere who seek to tackle racism while accusing the BBC of bias and irresponsibility. Yet whereas previous government utterances about race had usually come from hesitant white men anxious not to offend, now an assured black woman, unassailable to any charge of anti-black racism, was offering a forthright view without apology. Campaigners were on notice that many of their assumptions, until now unchallenged and glossed over for the sake of consensus, would not be accepted automatically. Badenoch had said that she regarded Britain as one of the best countries in which to be black, and her examination of variations in vulnerability to Covid would be sceptical about race as a determinant. A new chapter had begun.

Within twenty-four hours of her article appearing, a group of doctors surfaced to question the government's approach. In a letter sent jointly to Hancock and Badenoch, the doctors challenged the Public Health England report on the impact of coronavirus on ethnic minorities, calling it 'profoundly disappointing' for failing to address the root cause or propose any solutions. The authors said they were 'aghast' and were questioning 'the value – and even the intent' of the report. It was signed by the British Medical Association and groups representing medics from Ghanaian, Nigerian, Somali, Iraqi and Cameroonian backgrounds. One, JS Bamrah, the chairman of the British Association of Physicians of Indian Origin, labelled the report 'a half-baked job'. Another, Olamide Dada, representing African and Caribbean doctors, said it 'ignored the urgent need to protect Bame communities'. Badenoch explained the research had been 'conducted in a short period [and that it was] imperative that we understand the key drivers of those disparities'. She told the Commons that PHE had been unable to make any recommendations in its report because some of the data needed was unavailable.

Yet the campaigners' criticism was magnified by media suggestions that part of the report – one based on 4,000 personal testimonies from those in BAME communities – was being held back from public scrutiny. Professor Raj Bhopal of Edinburgh University, who had been asked to peer-review the unpublished recommendations, maintained that Parliament had 'not been told the full truth'. He suggested what he had seen bore 'every hallmark of a report ready to go to the press'. He went on: 'If you consult the public, you must publish the results. Otherwise, you've wasted their time, you've wasted your own time, you've wasted taxpayers' money and you've lost trust.'

In the event, the missing section, conducted by PHE's Professor Kevin Fenton, was published the following week. It concluded:

> Stakeholders pointed to racism and discrimination experienced by communities and more specifically BAME key workers as a root cause to exposure risk and disease progression … Racism and discrimination experienced by BAME key workers [is] a root cause affecting health and exposure risk. For BAME communities, lack of trust of NIIS services resulted in reluctance to seek care. It is clear from discussions with stakeholders the pandemic exposed and exacerbated longstanding inequalities affecting BAME communities in the UK.

Numerous theories were generated to explain the delay in publishing these findings. Censorship for fear of raising racial tensions was even cited in some not necessarily well-informed quarters. In fact, it was almost certainly a simple question of the report lacking full conclusions, even if Badenoch's own view seems to have been that the issue of race had been plentifully exploited, and that those who cried 'racism' had already received publicity. Whatever the truth, she, unusually, was on the back foot. At the very least, there had been a problem of presentation and her critics would be sure to see further evidence of racial health inequalities as proof of the government's failure to act when needed. A spokesman for the Department of Health delivered a comment that did little to settle the matter. 'More needs to be done,' this spokesman said. 'The equalities minister [Badenoch] is now undertaking further work to protect our communities from the impact of Covid-19.'

If Badenoch's muscular approach to the issue upset many campaigners, the attitude in Downing Street was more encouraging. Seemingly at the prompting of Munira Mirza, the head of the No. 10 policy unit, Boris Johnson let it be known that a new Commission on Race and Ethnic Disparities (CRED) would be set up to look at all aspects of racial and ethnic inequalities in Britain. Dr Tony Sewell, an international education consultant who ran the charity Generating Genius, which helps talented students from BAME backgrounds into higher education, would write the report. It was briefed that the commission would publish its findings by the end of the year, to Johnson himself, and would be overseen by Badenoch. Diane Abbott, the former shadow Home Secretary, was outraged. 'A new race equalities commission led by Munira Mirza is dead on arrival,' she complained. 'She has never believed in institutional racism.' Another Labour MP, David Lammy, called the plan a back-of-a-fag-packet effort. 'It feels that yet again in the UK we want figures, data, but we don't want action,' he alleged. 'Black people aren't playing victim, as Boris indicated – they are protesting precisely because the time for review is over and the time for action is now.'

Whether she liked it or not, in matters of identity politics Badenoch had become increasingly useful to the Conservatives as someone who could challenge a leftist sense of widespread racism in Britain without being accused of it herself. She is known to hate what some call 'grievance politics', and may therefore have preferred not to be drawn on the subject, but she spoke later of it being her 'duty' to play the role her party asked. That July, while giving evidence to the Commons Women and Equalities Committee, she admitted to being concerned about tokenism, so for somebody who wanted the world to be indifferent to skin colour, her high-profile utterances about race might have felt like a compromise. Specifically, she said she had already rejected one request by Johnson to answer questions about Covid and ethnicity at a televised press conference. 'I do think if it is done in the wrong way, it can look tokenistic,' she said.

> I was asked for instance at one point whether I would want to do a daily briefing, but I didn't feel, as a junior minister, that that would give the right impression. It would look like when we were talking about black issues we bring a black person on to talk about that, not about the wider things. I'm not just Equality Minister; I am also a Treasury Secretary. I think we also need to be very careful about giving the impression that ethnic minorities do ethnic subjects, women do women's subjects and everybody [else] does everything else.

She added:

> People shouldn't feel that advice has to come from people who look like them ... because if that happens, then the converse is true: where when an ethnic minority is speaking, people might feel well this person is only speaking for their sub-group. It is a challenge, that perception, but we shouldn't just accept it.

Despite having explained the complexities of her position as she saw it, she continued to be denounced for failing to tackle racism. David Isaac, the outgoing head of the Equality and Human Rights Commission, joined the chorus of people saying that further research was no answer. 'There are lots of people of colour who need supporting and for that reason a coherent race strategy is a top priority and I call upon the government to act urgently,' he said in an interview with the BBC. 'I do believe the government is dragging its feet ... The time for more recommendations in my view is over. We know what needs to be done. Let's get on with it. There are lots of quick wins such as implementing the ethnicity pay gap, for example.'

In response, Badenoch insisted that addressing racial inequality was a 'top priority'. Yet on the same day, she presented her detractors with a couple of damaging hostages following the arrest of a twelve-year-old boy in north London. The boy's mother, Alice Mina Agyepong, said her family felt 'utterly violated' and explained she had feared police would shoot her children when officers raided her home late at night and handcuffed her son. 'There must've been about twenty-five police officers, ten armed officers with weapons with red laser lights,' she told the *Camden New Journal*.

All I could see was police cars and lights. I told them almost straight away there were no weapons in the house, only a toy gun belonging to my son, but we were shouted at to put our hands above our heads and walk one by one out to the street. We were all terrified ... The whole time all I was thinking was: 'We're going to get shot.'

Their search recovered a plastic pellet gun.

On Radio 4's *Today* programme, Badenoch characteristically sought to downplay the relevance of race in the affair. 'I think it must be quite a frustrating and sensitive situation to find yourself in,' she acknowledged, before qualifying that statement

I have been in situations where I have been questioned by the police and at no point did I feel they were going to kill me ... I don't think we should be using this sort of language where people feel unarmed police officers try to kill people on the streets. We're hearing a lot of this rhetoric that is simply not true. We should not be trying to inflame tensions in this way by talking about police killing people when this is certainly not true.

From afar, it is hard to judge how much alarm it was reasonable for the Agyepong family to have felt, though it is striking that Badenoch's priority was to forestall any rise in racial tensions rather than to address the mother's feelings. Badenoch's own experience of being questioned by the police was taken up by Afua Hirsch of *The Guardian*, who used the episode to remind readers of other times when police had apparently mismanaged difficult situations. 'The presumption of innocence has always had racial caveats,' she wrote, chastising Badenoch for her expressed desire to 'reassure people about policing in this country'. To a large number of people in what some in government would call the 'race relations industry', Badenoch's attitude was simply complacent. Rarely can two factions of people claiming to want the same outcome – zero racism – have been so far apart. In any case, that same *Today* programme interview gave Badenoch an opportunity to trumpet some of her party's achievements, in defiance of claims about the government dragging its feet. She pointed out that the Lammy review of the criminal justice system in 2017, set up by Theresa May, had made thirty-five recommendations. 'We've already carried out sixteen of them,' she said.

I think there were only two out of thirty-five recommendations that we rejected and yet people act [as] if none of this work is happening ... One of the things that this race commission is doing is actually looking at – why is it that, despite all of these actions, people still believe that we're doing nothing? That's really important for me to work out.

On the HuffPost website, the headline on the story, written by reporter Nadine White, was 'New Race Commission "Was Set Up To Find Out Why People Think Tories Do Nothing On Racism"'. It was a form of words that was bound to enrage the minister being quoted and it appears to have sparked a squabble that had some way to run. As Badenoch's ally Lee Rowley MP explains:

There is a disconnect between Kemi and the media. The earliest interventions she became known for were around her equalities brief. And that challenged quite a lot of people in the metropolitan bubble, including quite a lot of journalists. There are quite a lot of people who write about her who aren't naturally predisposed to her. When she took on the concept of unconscious bias – which still has no real evidential basis – she did absolutely the right thing, but those who followed the liberal fashions didn't like it because it challenged their paradigm. I remember Black Lives Matter. I think many of us were unclear how to approach it at the time – we instinctively knew that a tragedy was being politicised by ideologues, but many of us didn't know how to articulate that. Kemi's willingness to speak truth on that was hugely important. Kemi was fearless in taking on things she knew weren't right. But that also meant that journalists incorrectly decided she was a 'culture warrior' because their first experience of her was about these hugely important issues. What they missed was that it was a thought-through broader political philosophy which underpinned what she was doing.

By late 2020, Britain had been subjected to months of bad news thanks to the coronavirus. While the speed of Covid's arrival might have made some early government mistakes forgivable in the public mind, other episodes undermined trust in officials' competence and sense of responsibility. During the first lockdown period, Boris Johnson's chief adviser, Dominic Cummings, had made a 260-mile trip from London to County Durham, breaching government rules in the process. Johnson decided to excuse this transgression. And in July 2020 it emerged that Johnson's own father, Stanley, had also made an unnecessary trip, this time to his holiday home in Greece. In addition to a suspicion that the crisis was being ineptly handled came a growing sense that while most of the country felt obliged to obey the government's rules, some Tories seemed to regard themselves as above the law.

Restrictions were lifted somewhat that summer before being reimposed in September. Most of the autumn was blighted by more deaths and limits on personal freedoms and economic activity. By October, some chinks of light began to appear, with signs that a viable vaccine might come to the rescue. Trials began and Badenoch was among those who signed up to take the Novavax jab. 'We have to ensure every community trusts a future vaccine to be safe and that it works across the entire population,' she said as she promoted it. 'But with less than half a per cent of people on the NHS Vaccine Registry from a black background, we have a lot more work to do.'

For her, nothing could be truer, as a barrage of awkward assertions was pumped out, each requiring her attention as the Equalities Minister. That month, a report from the Institute for Public Policy Research and Runnymede Trust think tanks concluded that the higher risk of death from Covid-19 among minority ethnic groups could not be explained by differences in underlying health conditions but, rather, unequal social conditions, unequal access to healthcare and 'structural and institutional racism'. The report said that 'urgent action' was necessary, arguing that when deciding who should have priority for limited Covid testing, ethnicity had to be considered as an independent risk factor alongside age, sex, occupation and underlying health conditions. Marsha de Cordova, Labour's shadow Equalities Minister, responded by alleging, 'Ministers' failure to prevent the disproportionate impact of Covid is negligent, discriminatory and unlawful.' Dr Chaand Nagpaul, council chair at the British Medical Association, said he was 'deeply concerned' that four months on from the publication of the PHE review, 35 per cent of intensive care beds were occupied by patients from BAME communities, and that twice as many ethnic minority people were infected by the virus. At around the same time, a report chaired by Baroness Lawrence, the mother of Stephen Lawrence who was murdered by racist thugs in south London in 1993, concluded that structural racism was responsible for the disproportionate impact of the coronavirus pandemic on BAME communities. Lady Lawrence's review found that BAME people were over-represented in public-facing industries, were more likely to live in overcrowded housing and were more likely to have been put at risk by the government's apparent failure to facilitate Covid-secure workplaces. 'This has been generations in the making,' she wrote. 'The impact of Covid is not random, but foreseeable and inevitable – the consequence of decades of structural injustice, inequality and discrimination that blights our society. We are in the middle of an avoidable crisis. And this report is a rallying cry to break that clear and tragic pattern.'

Some use a broad-brush approach to discern racism – whether institutional, structural or casual – in how society's inequalities affect the non-white population. Badenoch, however, defies any sense of the citizen being helpless or passive in the face of economic and other forces. Her conception of racism demands malign culprits rather than an ensemble of social variables. This approach was evident on 22 October when the first quarterly report of her Race Disparity Unit was published. It stated that most of the increased risk of infection and death from Covid-19 among people from ethnic minorities was explained by factors such as professional occupation, where people lived, their household composition and pre-existing health conditions, though it admitted that part of the excess risk remained unexplained in some groups such as black men and that further research was needed.

Speaking on behalf of the report, Dr Raghib Ali, a senior clinical research associate at Cambridge University's MRC Epidemiology Unit who had accepted a new job as a government adviser on Covid and ethnicity, steered reporters away from the idea of ethnicity being responsible. 'It's not that [ethnic minority people] won't be at increased risk – we will still have those risk factors, but we have to address the risk factors rather than just saying it's ethnicity,' he said. 'We didn't have all this information at the beginning, so it was reasonable to use ethnicity as a proxy early on. But now we need to extend it to the whole population.' Dr Ali said he saw no evidence that structural racism had contributed to the higher risk of infection and death in ethnic minorities (which Public Health England had suggested in its June report), noting that the PHE paper relied on the perceptions of 4,000 stakeholders rather than objective evidence.

If structural racism was an important problem – I'm not saying it doesn't exist – but if it was an important problem in health outcomes then you'd expect that to be reflected not just in Covid but in other outcomes as well. There is certainly no evidence from either the ONS [Office for National Statistics] paper or the OpenSafely data that blacks and south Asians were treated any differently once they reached hospital. I don't think structural racism is a reasonable explanation. Those that put it forward need to provide evidence.

In the same week, Badenoch took part in a six-hour parliamentary debate to mark Black History Month. She used the occasion to declare that the Conservatives were opposed to critical race theory – the idea that Western societies are inherently biased towards white people – and to criticise Black Lives Matter. 'We do not want teachers to teach their white pupils about white privilege and inherited racial guilt,' she told the Commons. 'Any school which teaches these elements of critical race theory, or which promotes partisan political views such as defunding the police without offering a balanced treatment of opposing views, is breaking the law.' In fact, according to insiders, she adopted this position without the sanction of Boris Johnson, who was instinctively reluctant to engage in matters relating to cultural or racial politics. 'Boris did not like all this stuff,' says one insider.

> He was squeamish. [His now wife] Carrie hated this anti-woke agenda and didn't want the Tories to fight in this arena. Kemi did want to fight, so she was in constant tension with him about whether the Conservatives were going to do this or not. Remember, he was PM when Penny Mordaunt was saying trans men are men and trans women are women, and that seemed to be accepted. Kemi went rogue and committed the Tories to a position

on critical race theory. The Red Wall people loved it, but No. 10 didn't like it at all.

A friend adds:

> She does worry about typecasting. She hates the argument that only black people can talk about these things. She'll say, 'Look at the hassle I get, you should talk about it as well.' But the fact is she's good at this stuff and if you're going to attack wokery, a black mother is extremely well placed to do it because she doesn't want her own children being given this patronising treatment and told that their history is slavery, which is not necessarily the Nigerian experience. It might be the Caribbean experience, but it's not the African experience. She says there are statues of slave traders in Nigeria who are still revered.

She followed up the debate by giving an interview to her former boss at *The Spectator*, Fraser Nelson. 'Many people don't realise that [critical race theory] is political,' she said. 'It's getting into institutions that really should be neutral: schools, NHS trusts and even sometimes the civil service.' She also lashed out at books such as *White Fragility* by Robin DiAngelo and *Why I'm No Longer Talking To White People About Race* by Reni Eddo-Lodge which support such claims. 'Many of these books – and, in fact, some of the authors and proponents of critical race theory – actually want a segregated society,' she told Nelson. And yet, she noted, big corporations and public institutions seemed to be supportive of ideas such as unconscious bias. She had clearly thought about the issue quite deeply. 'The logical conclusion of what they're saying is that people in Africa who are not discriminated against on the basis of their race are not really black,' she said. 'It is associating being black with negativity, oppression and victimhood in an inescapable way. It's creating a prison for black people.'

Her claim that proponents of critical race theory want a segregated society was swiftly challenged. More than 100 black writers, including Bernardine Evaristo, Malorie Blackman, Benjamin Zephaniah and other members of the Black Writers' Guild wrote in *The Guardian*:

> The allegation here is not only clearly false, but dangerous. It risks endangering the personal safety of anti-racist writers. In recent years progressive writers, politicians and activists across Europe and the United Kingdom have been physically attacked and killed by far-right extremists … It is in this climate that we ask the government to ensure ministers are responsible with their language, avoid spreading misinformation and apply better judgment in order to protect the lives and freedom of minorities.

In the same *Spectator* interview, she was unapologetic about not trying to meet her opponents halfway. When it was put to her by Nelson that her own party had dabbled in '[the equalities agenda] for quite some time, talking up racial injustice, then posing as the avengers', she replied:

> In trying to show that you are a party representing all people, you accept some of the false rhetoric in order to be able to demonstrate that you're doing something about it. But there are enough problems for us without having to create new ones … The repetition of the victimhood narrative is really poisonous for young people because they hear it and believe it.

Her philosophical position on race was most eloquently expressed in summing up the aforementioned six-hour-long Black History Month debate. Given the seriousness of the issue, and the fact that it was voted the Speech of the Year 2020 by the ConservativeHome website, it is worth quoting at length.

> What we are against is the teaching of contested political ideas as if they are accepted facts. We do not do that with communism, socialism or capitalism. I want to speak about a dangerous trend in race relations that has come far too close to home in my life, which is the promotion of critical race theory, an ideology that sees my blackness as victimhood and their whiteness as oppression. I want to be absolutely clear that the government stand unequivocally against critical race theory. Some schools have decided to openly support the anti-capitalist Black Lives Matter group, often fully aware that they have a statutory duty to be politically impartial. Of course black lives matter, but we know that the Black Lives Matter movement is political. I know that because, at the height of the protests, I have been told of white Black Lives Matter protesters calling a black armed police officer guarding Downing Street – I apologise for saying this word – 'a pet nigger'. That is why we do not endorse that movement on this side of the House. It is a political movement. It would be nice if opposition members condemned many of the actions of that political movement, instead of pretending that it is a completely wholesome anti-racist organisation...
>
> Our history is our own; it is not America's. Too often, those who campaign against racial inequality import wholesale a narrative and assumptions that have nothing to do with this country's history and have no place on these islands ... Most black British

people who came to our shores were not brought here in chains but came voluntarily because of their connections to the UK and in search of a better life. I should know: I am one of them. We have our own joys and sorrows to tell. From the Windrush generation to the Somali diaspora, it is a story that is uniquely ours. If we forget that story and replace it with an imported Americanised narrative of slavery, segregation and Jim Crow, we erase the history of not only black Britain but every other community that has contributed to society and that has also been a victim of racism or discrimination, from the Pakistani community to the Jewish community …

Why does this issue mean so much to me? It is not just because I am a first-generation immigrant. It is because my daughter came home from school this month and said to me, 'We're learning Black History Month because every other month is about white history.' That is wrong and it is not what our children should be picking up. Those are not the values that I have taught her. They are yet another sign of the pernicious identity politics that look at individuals primarily as groups of biological characteristics …

History tells us that this is a country that welcomes people, and that black people from all over the world have found this to be a great and welcoming country. As a black woman, these are the values that I am teaching my black daughter. We must never take that for granted. In this Black History Month, let us celebrate the black talent that we are blessed with, the progress we have made in accepting one another and the contribution that black people have made in making us who we are as a nation.

Her outspokenness laid the ground for yet more news stories about disharmony among anti-racists. For example, Halima Begum, the recently appointed director of the Runnymede Trust race equalities think tank, accused the government of pursuing a divisive 'white nationalist' agenda to secure white working-class votes at the expense of ethnic minorities. 'What we should be saying is that working-class black and white communities have been left behind,' she said,

> because they've seen industries demolished. We haven't seen the economies built back, we haven't seen investment in our education system for years so that our black, white and Asian working-class children will thrive. What I see instead is the Conservatives pushing through [a narrative of] a white working class that's been left behind, which is where [Donald] Trump was at about six years ago.

What followed was trickier. In late January 2021, the government put out a video designed to encourage those from ethnic minorities to sign up for the new Covid vaccine. Nadine White, the reporter for the HuffPost news website whose headline had angered Badenoch the previous year, contacted her to ask why she did not appear alongside other ethnic minority MPs in the video. Badenoch posted eight tweets criticising White, who then received some abusive messages as a result. Badenoch accused the HuffPost of 'looking to sow distrust by making up claims I refused to take part in a video campaign', saying of White it was a 'sad insight into how some journalists operate' and calling her behaviour 'creepy and bizarre'. This reaction was considered by some to be disproportionate and it brought demands from senior officials for an explanation. There was even talk of the ministerial code having been broken. And it did not help her case that White, who is black, had lost her older sister to Covid three weeks earlier, as well as a cousin and friends the previous year. Yet White can scarcely be described as an entirely dispassionate seeker of the truth. Previously, she had claimed – inaccurately – that Badenoch had suggested 'racism isn't an issue in the UK' and tweeted critically about Badenoch nine times before the row over the video.

The spat brought another critic out of the shadows. Samuel Kasumu, Boris Johnson's adviser on civil society and community since 2019, wrote a letter of resignation to the Prime Minister. In the event, he was persuaded by the Tory MP Nadhim Zahawi to withdraw it, though its contents reached the media. It said the attack by Badenoch, with whom he said he had no personal difficulties, was 'not OK and not justifiable … The damage that is often caused by our actions is not much considered.' He said later:

> I thought to myself: if that young journalist was my sister, or a relative of mine, how would I feel about a minister responding to her in such a way? If the journalist was Andrew Neil, or Laura Kuenssberg, or Robert Peston, would the minister have responded in the same way? Were the minister's actions distracting people from very important public health messages? And all of those things, and a few other things, just led me to the conclusion that it was completely unacceptable.

Few others in Downing Street seemed concerned by Badenoch's behaviour, though. Kasumu said he 'waited, and waited, for something from the senior leadership team to even point to an expected standard, but it did not materialise'. The closest to criticism that anyone managed was from the press office, which said, 'This would not be how we in No. 10 deal with these things.' The Cabinet Office later dismissed a complaint from HuffPost.

Johnson's apparent tolerance was criticised by Lord Woolley, a former chairman of the race disparity unit in Whitehall, who said he should force Badenoch to apologise or sack her. 'I hope that Samuel's bravery in calling this out provokes a true leadership response. Unless Kemi Badenoch offers a fulsome apology to Nadine White, her position appears to be untenable,' Woolley said.

> This is a critical moment for the government. A key black special adviser in No. 10 Downing Street is deeply concerned about the politics of division. Samuel Kasumu is referring to the government's strategy that pits poor white people against poor black people, for example by rubbishing Black Lives Matter and arguing that class in the northern regions, a code for white working class, is a greater inequality than racism. What Kasumu and others want is for the government to about-face and radically begin to acknowledge and deal with the deep-seated racial inequalities that have been laid bare by Covid-19 such as jobs, health and housing.

This may have shown what forces Badenoch was up against, but no resignation followed.

In January 2021, the minister in charge of Covid vaccine deployment, Nadhim Zahawi, wrote an article in *The Sun* celebrating its rapid and extensive rollout. At that point, with the elderly and infirm being given priority, nearly 8 million people had had their first jab. But, wrote Zahawi at his most upbeat, 'while most of us are willing to take vaccines, some small pockets of the community are more hesitant'. He acknowledged that 10 to 20 per cent of ethnic minority communities were less likely to take the vaccine and said he was making a priority of regularly meeting faith leaders and inaccessible groups to counter scare stories and concerns about the safety of Covid vaccines.

A Scientific Advisory Group for Emergencies study had revealed that almost three quarters of black Britons (71.8 per cent) were unlikely or very unlikely to get the jab, while black and ethnic minority communities were up to twice as likely to die from Covid as white people. The same study revealed 42.3 per cent of Pakistani and Bangladeshi Brits were unlikely to get the jab, while 84.8 per cent of white Britons wanted to be vaccinated. 'We must expose the anti-vaxxer disinformation peddled by those who have nothing better to do than scaremonger,' Badenoch said. 'It is risking lives and causing harmful, unnecessary division in our society.' A separate study published in late February showed a significant cut in mortality rates among people who identify as black African between the first and second Covid waves the previous year, but in the second wave the Pakistani and Bangladeshi community had the highest deaths per 100,000 of any minority. Badenoch took the opportunity of saying that the findings showed that 'it is completely inaccurate to categorise all minority ethnic people into one homogenous group – and potentially damaging if the measures we take are designed to fit that narrative'.

It was not long before Kasumu, Badenoch and Woolley were in the news again. In March 2021, four months after it was originally expected, the 264-page report by the Commission of Race and Ethnic Disparities – a body which Woolley had previously called a 'motley crew of deniers' – was published. Its outcome would not have surprised Woolley. Written by Dr Tony Sewell, who was well disposed towards Badenoch, the report concluded there was no evidence of institutional racism in Britain. Instead, it found that geography, family influence, socio-economic background, culture and religion all impact life chances more than racism. While admitting that disparities remain in senior public and private sector posts, Sewell maintained that the overall picture was improving and that law and medicine were increasingly diverse. The pay gap between ethnic minority and white employees had shrunk to 2.3 per cent and had virtually disappeared among workers aged under thirty, said the report. Among its recommendations was the scrapping of the term 'BAME' on the grounds that it is outdated and fails to distinguish between different groups.

The report sought to strike a more soothing tone than the one that had recently characterised the debate around racial issues, even if it was occasionally blunt. For example, one section spelled out a fallacy Badenoch had been keen to nail. It read: 'The idea that all ethnic minority people suffer a common fate and a shared disadvantage is an anachronism.' It made a few concessions to its anticipated critics.

We understand the idealism of those well-intentioned young people who have held on to, and amplified, inter-generational mistrust. However, we also have to ask whether a narrative that claims nothing has changed for the better, and that the dominant feature of our society is institutional racism and White privilege, will achieve anything beyond alienating the decent centre ground – a centre ground which is occupied by people of all races and ethnicities.

It continued:

This Commission finds that the big challenge of our age is not overt racial prejudice, it is building on and advancing the progress won by the struggles of the past 50 years. This requires us to take a broader, dispassionate look at what has been holding some people back. We therefore cannot accept the accusatory tone of much of the current rhetoric on race, and the pessimism about what has been and what more can be achieved.

Yet the accusatory attitude was not to be banished so easily. On social media Sewell was likened both to the Nazi propagandist Joseph Goebbels and to the Ku Klux Klan. The University of Nottingham later said that because of the 'political controversy' over the report, it was withdrawing its offer of awarding Sewell an honorary degree. Less contentiously, one of the eleven commissioners said the government was guilty of 'bending' its work to fit a political narrative. Another commissioner, anti-racism activist Kunle Olulode, said that the report did not show enough understanding of institutional or structural discrimination and came to conclusions based on 'selective' use of evidence. But No. 10 denied this while confirming that commissioners had not seen the whole report before it was published.

Two researchers named in the report disassociated themselves from it. Historian Stephen Bourne said he was 'duped' by No. 10 into attending a discussion without being told about the commission or its work. And S. I. Martin, a writer and historian, said he found out to his 'horror' that he was listed as a stakeholder. He told the BBC: 'I have absolutely no association with the commission. The document attempts to press a sort of veneer of respectability on what are quite odious and divisive politics.' More than 100 Windrush campaigners signed a joint letter urging Sewell to ditch the report, which they accused of denying the experiences of hundreds of black British citizens who had been unlawfully stripped of their right to live and work in the UK. One source on the commission told *The Observer*,

'Basic fundamentals in putting a document like this together were ignored. When you're producing something so historic, you have to avoid unnecessary controversy; you don't court it like this report did. And the comms was just shocking.'

Nadine White wrote a characteristically forceful piece saying the government was manipulating ethnic minority communities by suggesting that institutional racism is imaginary. 'Anecdotally, virtually everyone from within ethnic minority communities have spoken of very real lived experiences of grappling with the same sort of ingrained discrimination – and yet this report does not acknowledge this,' she wrote. She expressed particular outrage over 'one of the most stunning segments', which attempted to 'put a positive spin on slavery', quoting the report's foreword, which said: 'There is a new story about the Caribbean experience which speaks to the slave period not only being about profit and suffering but how culturally African people transformed themselves into a re-modelled African/Britain.' Again, little common ground was likely to emerge between an angry journalist wanting to lighten hardship and improve the world and a government mindset whose default recommendation on the issue might come across as 'lighten up'. Following wider criticism, that section of the report was later amended to say: 'This is to say that in the face of the inhumanity of slavery, African people preserved their humanity and culture. This includes the story of slave resistance.'

In March 2021, the BBC broadcast a documentary presented by the actor David Harewood called *Why Is Covid Killing People of Colour?* In it, he asked why, as a 55-year-old man, he was three times more likely to die of Covid than a white man of the same age. He learned that 95 per cent of doctors who had died from Covid were from ethnic minority backgrounds and explored a possible Vitamin

D deficiency among those with darker skins. He also confronted Badenoch, who told him: 'It is not skin colour that causes the problem; it is underlying risks.' He, like many others, pointed to systemic racism. And he concluded by considering how the inequalities exposed by Covid-19 and the Black Lives Matter movement had come together at a pivotal time which could result in change. Slightly less predictable was the decision of Samuel Kasumu to submit his resignation, and this time he stood by it. The government claimed the timing had nothing to do with the Sewell report, though it could hardly have been a coincidence.

Harewood's film was aired two weeks before the Sewell report appeared, perhaps with Sewell's findings in mind. The report covered a lot of ground and included many, but not all, opinions across the spectrum. If it sought to create converts, win hearts and minds and set the nation pulling in the same direction, it failed. If the attempt was to stir up controversy and promote 'culture wars' friction, as some have suggested, arguably it succeeded. Isabel Hardman, writing in *The Observer*, summed up the view of many journalists when she opined that most Conservatives thought there was a deliberate strategy from No. 10 to ensure 'there was a drawn-out row about [the report's] conclusions'. Hardman claimed that Munira Mirza and Badenoch felt that 'the only way to make genuine progress on racial equality is to go on a clear offensive against the shibboleths of the left', adding: 'They are happy to have this period of fighting – characterised as the "war on woke" – in the hope it will enable the government to really move on, rather than endlessly getting stuck in the weeds on ground held by the left.'

More than ever, Badenoch was perceived as playing the role of Boris Johnson's licensed pugilist on race. Yet, apart from being emotionally draining for her, to say nothing of disrupting her other duties as a minister and MP, it may well have come at a personal cost. It later emerged that in September 2021 she called upon the help of Jeremy Hildreth, a brand consultant and protégé of the celebrated corporate branding guru Wally Olins. According to Badenoch's parliamentary declaration of interests, Hildreth provided 'legal research and advice on online abuse, harassment and intimidation'. Though given in kind, it was valued at £26,755.20. Hildreth has advised all sorts of clients, 'from banks and barbecue grill makers, to nations and neighbourhoods, to airlines and armies', though he is not a lawyer. The precise nature of the assistance he gave to Badenoch is unclear, though it is hard to imagine a department more likely to attract online trolling than Badenoch's.

On a personal level, there was another development that turned out to be devastating. During the summer of 2021, Badenoch learned that her father, Femi, had a brain tumour. He died in January 2022. At the time of his death, she posted a tribute to him on Twitter. 'I cried more times in the last five months than I did the 40 years before,' she wrote.

> It's been agony coming to terms with what I knew was coming. No matter how much I prepared, I still wasn't ready to let him go. I'm grateful for everything he taught me, for the time we had together, for his being such a great dad and for helping me become the woman I am today. Nothing will ever be the same again. Rest in peace, Daddy.

Her words were accompanied by a photograph of her as a little girl with her father.

Her brother, Folahan, says, 'In his last few days, my father often said he knew Kemi would do more and keep rising and he cried knowing he would not be there to see it.' It must have been bit-tersweet for the family to realise that Badenoch's father had been right. Just a few months after his death, his daughter would gain new prominence as her political career advanced.

CHAPTER 9

AN UNEXPECTED ADVENTURE

In mid-September 2021, Boris Johnson decided to enact a ministerial reshuffle. Kemi Badenoch had been confidently tipped by most lobby journalists to replace Gavin Williamson as Education Secretary. As it turned out, she remained Minister for Equalities and was also appointed, somewhat confusingly, Minister of State (Foreign, Commonwealth and Development Office) (jointly with Department for Levelling Up, Housing and Communities), in which capacity she would be working closely with Michael Gove. In fact, her tenure in these posts lasted only a matter of months, as Johnson's grip on power weakened.

Johnson's woes began in earnest in November 2021 when he was badly advised in trying to defend Owen Paterson, a former Tory Cabinet minister who had been found guilty by the parliamentary authorities of breaking lobbying rules. In a doomed bid to save Paterson's career, Johnson instructed MPs to vote for reform of the parliamentary standards watchdog, which would, he hoped, allow certain rules to be swerved. The scheme was quickly exposed by MPs across the House of Commons as morally squalid. Paterson resigned and Johnson's reputation was depleted – doubly so when Paterson's Shropshire seat was lost in the resulting by-election with a 34 per cent swing from the Conservatives to the Liberal Democrats.

At the end of November 2021, the *Daily Mirror* published the first of many stories alleging that parties had been taking place at 10 Downing Street during lockdown, in breach of rules that the nation had been expected to follow. In January 2022, at Prime Minister's Questions, Johnson confirmed that he had indeed attended a party in the No. 10 garden during the first lockdown in May 2020 and he offered a 'heartfelt apology'. It was the sort of tangle into which he had long been drawn, and few believed the matter would end there. The media had a new bone to chew.

Badenoch attempted to get on with business as usual and early in the new year she made an appearance in the *Daily Telegraph*, this time attacking social media giants for allowing fake news to spread. Statistics showed that almost one fifth of the most critically ill Covid-19 patients were expectant mothers who had not received their first jab. 'Equally alarming', she wrote, was that 'only 5.5 per cent of pregnant black women were vaccinated, despite clear evidence that this group is more likely to be hospitalised with Covid.' She admitted that initially pregnant women had been advised not to have the jab, but the evidence was now crystal clear: 'the vaccine is safe for pregnant women'. Pregnant women were more likely to fall seriously ill with Covid-19 than non-pregnant women of the same age, and Covid-19 in pregnancy was linked to a higher risk of premature delivery. She issued a vigorous call for all pregnant women to ignore antivax rhetoric and have the jab. However, the focus of most people's attention in Westminster was on what had by now come to be known in the press as 'Partygate'. Predictably, Johnson's apology had not been sufficient for Sue Gray, the senior civil servant who had been asked to investigate the allegations. She observed in an interim report published on 31 January: 'At least some of the gatherings in question represent a serious failure to observe not just the high standards expected of those working at the heart of Government but also of the standards expected of the entire British population at the time.' The report added that 'a number of these gatherings should not have been allowed to take place or to develop in the way that they did. There is significant learning to be drawn from these events which must be addressed immediately across Government.'

Further embarrassment for Johnson followed that day. After once again apologising to the House, he and Sir Keir Starmer began a debate in which Johnson attacked the Labour leader over his five-year record as the Director of Public Prosecutions, criticising him for having spent 'more time prosecuting journalists and failing to prosecute Jimmy Savile'. The director of the No. 10 policy unit, Munira Mirza – a close ally of Badenoch – told him he should apologise, but he refused, resulting in her resignation. Few believed Mirza's decision was based solely on the Savile remark. Rather, it was taken as evidence of general frustration with his leadership. Within hours, three other senior aides had followed suit.

Not long afterwards, in March 2022, Badenoch published the government's initial response to the Sewell report of nearly a year earlier. It seems that, beyond merely challenging her opponents' comfortable assumptions, she genuinely saw this as work that she needed to confront as best she could. As her fellow 2017 entrant to Parliament Rachel Maclean says:

She really cares about why things are the way they are. With Kemi, it's not just about getting a quick win and moving on. It's more a case of 'How do we really think about this problem facing the country and what will we do to solve it?' That has always been the way she's approached everything.

Entitled 'Inclusive Britain', the report was a less antagonistic and more practical look at how racial disparities might be addressed. It stated that the way forward was not to 'decolonise this, tear down that', nor to 'get civil servants to read books on white privilege or worry about statues in Oxford colleges'. It said that social mobility among minority communities was improving and that where 'persistent disparities between ethnic groups do exist', they were 'more likely to be caused by factors other than racism and discrimination'. A 74-point plan was unveiled that sought to avoid pitting people against each other. It advised schools and colleges to be 'careful' about using terms like 'white privilege' and recommended increasing trust between police and minority communities. It advocated helping first-time drug offenders in order to avoid them joining a cycle of crime. A new 'model history curriculum' for schools would foster inclusion by telling the story of the making of modern Britain. The government would appoint a 'diverse' panel of historians to develop it by 2024 to support high-quality teaching of Britain's 'complex' past. Stop-and-search laws would be amended, police forces and the judiciary would become more representative and ethnic minorities would receive improved legal advice when in police custody. Firms would be encouraged to do more to tackle pay disparities between white employees and those of other races, and thirty-seven 'progression champions' would support children from ethnic communities to get on in life. Racism online would be challenged and public sector training on diversity and inclusion would be amended. It also promised that government and public sector bodies would stop using the term BAME because it was 'poorly understood' and obscured 'important disparities between different ethnic groups'.

The verdict of *The Guardian* was that it was an improvement on the Sewell report itself, though the newspaper claimed Badenoch shared 'its authors' determination to take a broadly positive view of multicultural Britain'. It found several elements to applaud and appeared to recognise the more conciliatory approach. Yet it warned that some plans were vague, rounding off its editorial comment as follows:

> There is no sign of the resources that the NHS will need if it is to reduce health inequalities, or of the poverty-reduction strategy that would underpin any serious move in this direction. Educational inequalities are widening rather than narrowing. Against this backdrop, it is hard to believe that 'inclusive Britain' will amount to more than warm words.

The contrast between the largely civil exchanges in Westminster and the reality of everyday life on Britain's streets was immediately evident at that time. As if to rebuke any complacency, the media reported that day that a fifteen-year-old black girl, who for legal reasons was known as Child Q, had been strip-searched at her school. Her lawyers announced that she was going to take civil action against the Metropolitan Police and the school. She was said to be acting to obtain 'cast-iron commitments to ensure this never happens again to any other child'. In the House of Commons, Badenoch called it an 'appalling incident'. She welcomed the police's apology and said the case would be investigated by the Independent Office for Police Conduct. She added:

What we cannot do is stop any bad thing from happening to anyone in the country at any time. But what we do know is that everybody is rightly appalled and outraged by what happened to Child Q. That is an example of a country that cares about ethnic minorities and about children in the system, and we will continue to do everything we can to support them.

In an interview looking back on that period, Badenoch once again lamented the media's unwillingness to report her arguments more sympathetically. 'There's so much political activism in this space and it's very hard to get heard,' she told *The Spectator*.

So many people are scared to talk about these issues because they get attacked ... We've created a situation where if you're white you're not allowed to talk about race. You have to defer to people of a different colour ... I think that is wrong and I am hopefully doing enough to create that space so we can all have that conversation.

In June 2022, she made another characteristically controversial decision, this time one that might have been designed to rile transgender activists, though it was not announced for some weeks. New office buildings, schools, hospitals and entertainment venues would have to have separate male and female lavatories. The days of gender-neutral facilities were gone. She had acted after being warned that some children were avoiding using lavatories at school because they only had access to shared facilities, not single-sex ones. It was a very Badenochian issue, though she denied being needlessly argumentative. 'No, I would not cross the road to pick a fight,' she told the *Spectator* podcast, 'but I do not shy away from confrontation because politics is where we are meant to deal with difficult decisions. If a decision was easy then it doesn't need politics.' Trans rights was an issue to which she would return.

The full version of Sue Gray's final report, published at the end of May 2022, confirmed that senior Downing Street officials, both political and non-political, bore responsibility for the culture of partying during Covid lockdowns. Johnson's version of events looked threadbare, and by the weekend of the Queen's Platinum Jubilee celebrations in early June, thirty Conservative MPs had said publicly that he should quit. Those who submitted a letter of no confidence in his leadership quickly swelled to a group of more than fifty-four – or 15 per cent of the parliamentary party – the figure needed to force a vote on his future. This secret ballot took place on Monday 6 June. Johnson received 211 votes – or 59 per cent of the parliamentary party – while 148 MPs voted against him. At the height of her difficulties in 2018, Theresa May had done better. History does not relate on which side Badenoch came down, but Johnson had the backing of more than half of his parliamentary party and under party rules could, in theory, survive for another twelve months unchallenged. In practice, however, he would have known that the game was almost up.

In fact, an unexpected catalyst ultimately brought his premiership to an end. After allegedly groping two men in the Carlton Club while he was drunk, Chris Pincher MP, a Johnson loyalist, resigned as Deputy Chief Whip on 30 June. Further allegations were then aired about Pincher's behaviour and questions were asked about his past conduct in light of his purported out-of-hours record. Johnson had claimed that he had not known of specific allegations against Pincher before appointing him to a Foreign Office job in 2019. Exceptionally, though, Lord McDonald, a former Foreign Office civil servant, stated publicly that he had evidence proving that Johnson knew more about Pincher than he seemed to have suggested. On the afternoon of 5 July, Johnson gave an emergency interview to the BBC in which he said that he 'bitterly' regretted not acting on the information he had received about Pincher. An hour later, Sajid Javid, the Health Secretary, resigned. Nine minutes after that, Rishi Sunak, the Chancellor, also left the government. Over the following two days, sixty other ministers and officials followed suit. The Prime Minister's integrity and ability to command his party's respect were shot. On 7 July, he announced that he would stand down.

In the months leading up to this seismic event, Badenoch had been watching the government unravel with the same sense of trepidation as many of her colleagues. Having reconnected with a coterie of MPs from the 2017 intake, it was clear that she was not alone in harbouring serious doubts about the direction in which the parliamentary party, and the country, had moved under Johnson. The group would meet periodically to share their concerns and swap ideas about a range of matters. 'We'd debate all sorts of things,' says one member of this circle, Julia Lopez.

> We worried about the increasing disconnect between the public and politicians. We were wondering about the post-Covid world in terms of public expenditure. We would discuss cultural issues. So we naturally came together. There was a bit of a generational shift within the party. People were starting to get junior ministerial positions and starting to understand how the system works and how you might want to change the system. It was a gathering of like-minded colleagues and we were also friends. You need friends in politics. We wanted to formulate a factual, as opposed to an emotional, response.

As 2022 wore on, one of their chief worries was Johnson himself. 'We were all concerned about the leadership and how No. 10 was being run,' says Lopez.

> You could see it was chaotic. What were our guiding principles? You have to bear in mind – every time something negative hap-pens you get a hit from your constituents. In holding the line, you have to defend something you're not comfortable with yourself, but you contrast that against the mandate of the PM, the dem-ocratic consent he holds, particularly post-2019 when we had a big majority, and you have to try to disaggregate the concerns of the Westminster bubble versus what your constituents think and work out where the majority of the public are versus where you are personally, so you're trying to decide 'At what point does this become untenable?'

On the evening of 5 July 2022, Lopez and a few others – including Badenoch – met and agreed they were all 'unhappy' under John-son's leadership. They decided to go away and think about things individually and then meet in Lopez's parliamentary office the fol-lowing morning. 'I tried to write a resignation letter overnight,' says Lopez. 'It didn't work.' They concluded that a joint letter of resig-nation would be appropriate. It stated that it had been an 'honour' to serve in Johnson's administration and that he had 'had the most difficult task in a generation', but it made clear their belief that the government 'cannot function given the issues that have come to light and the way in which they have been handled' and called on him to tender his resignation. It was written and signed by Baden-och, Lopez, Lee Rowley, Alex Burghart and Neil O'Brien. 'We didn't want to humiliate Boris ahead of PMQs, so we told the Chief Whip

[Chris Heaton-Harris] and he showed the letter to the PM ahead of his appearance in front of the Liaison Committee that afternoon,' explains Lopez. 'The Chief Whip met us at two o'clock and said, "Boris is fighting on", so we resigned at about 2.15.'

Badenoch published a copy of the letter that afternoon on her Twitter account, explaining, 'With great regret, I resigned from the government this morning. It has been an honour being Equalities and Local Government minister. It was a privilege to have worked with so many great ministerial colleagues and civil servants in these roles.' Five ministerial departures in one fell swoop had the immediate effect of convincing some journalists that this faction might represent the future of the post-Johnson Conservative Party. Reporters were not the only ones who had begun to think in those terms. 'We talked through the options,' remembers Lopez.

> We talked about whether one of us should think about standing. There was reticence. Kemi didn't put herself forward and I think on the Thursday [7 July] she said maybe she'd consider it. Lee and I said, 'Are you serious, because we would consider backing you but only if you did it to win, not half-heartedly.'

This was hardly outlandish talk. Senior Tories including Ruth Davidson, the former leader of the Scottish Conservatives, had publicly singled out Badenoch as a 'sober' alternative to Johnson the previous year.

Behind the scenes – and perhaps unknown to close allies like Lopez and Rowley – Badenoch was that day involved in what some of Johnson's most ardent supporters have portrayed as a piece of skulduggery. Within hours of quitting, she sent a message in a

WhatsApp ministerial group chat to Sarah Dines, at that time an assistant government whip, which read: 'Resign before midnight. DO IT. DO IT. DO IT.' It was accompanied by a laughing emoji. The WhatsApp group had by then been renamed 'DLUHC ex?Ministers Group' (DLUHC standing for Department for Levelling Up, Housing and Communities). Badenoch had also begun thinning out the group, removing from it two other ministers, Eddie Hughes and Lord Greenhalgh, who remained in their government posts. It was later reported that when she began this process of deletion, an adviser to Michael Gove wrote: 'The others can stay if they stay quiet.' Despite Badenoch's message, Dines did not resign and the episode remained out of the spotlight until early 2023, when the message was leaked by a supporter of Boris Johnson to the *Mail on Sunday*, encouraging some MPs at that point to question Badenoch's true motives. It is worth saying that Dines did, however, end up supporting Badenoch in the ensuing leadership contest.

The evening of 7 July 2022 was feverish. Not only was the temperature blazing but the *Spectator* garden party was also taking place at the magazine's headquarters in Old Queen Street, Westminster, an event to which every significant player in the Conservative Party was invited. Anybody who was there will remember it as a strange occasion in which private succession plans were being hatched in this semi-public setting. Rishi Sunak and his team were to be found in one corner of the garden while another candidate, Nadhim Zahawi, was in another with his band of cheerleaders. A third candidate, Tom Tugendhat, who had announced his candidacy that day, was also milling around in the hope of picking up support. Lopez, Badenoch and Rowley decided to attend as well in order to see who else was likely to put themselves forward. 'I think there was a concern from other camps that Kemi would run,' reflects Lopez. 'They didn't want her to. Various conversations took place. People were trying to talk her out of it.'

And yet others present were apparently far more positive about her chances. Rowley takes up the story.

There is this assumption that Kemi's been after the leadership since the beginning. Since I've known her well, that's not the case. The resignation decision was extremely difficult for us all and it was entirely about doing what she, and we, thought was right. It was never about leadership. We never discussed that. Yet, after Boris quit, there was a general lack of enthusiasm for the options coming forward and we said to each other, 'If we don't like any of the options, who else is going to give it a go?' But Kemi was very reluctant. I remember we were going to the *Spectator* party and that was the night she decided. I had said to her, 'I really think you should have a go because of the lot of us, you're the one who has done a lot of thinking about things.' She wasn't convinced. I remember in my office before we went I said, 'You're going to have to make a decision and I really think you should do it.' Julia was there. After the party we linked up and she said, 'I don't want to do it, but I think I should do it, I think it's important that I do it, it's important there's a choice.'

Lopez adds:

We'd heard some positive feedback at the party. If there'd been an obvious successor to Boris, he'd have gone sooner. Among us, Kemi was the only person who'd worked with both Liz and Rishi closely as she'd been a junior minister in the Equalities and

Treasury departments. She always said they'd be found out under pressure and that was why people needed more choice. We felt it was important to show we wanted to try and do things differently. I want to bust this idea this is something she'd been plotting for years. It was us trying to persuade her to think about doing it because one of us had to give it a bash, just to show there were more options than people thought.

Badenoch had never been a Cabinet minister, she did not have the highest political profile in the party and, unlike some of the other candidates who were limbering up to succeed Johnson, no proper preparations for her campaign had been made by this stage. To complicate matters further, it seems there had been a hope in the minds of Badenoch's supporters that Suella Braverman might pair up with her and pitch herself as Badenoch's deputy. This idea went down in flames when Braverman unexpectedly announced her intention to stand for the leadership herself the night before the *Spectator* party, during an appearance on the ITV programme *Peston*. 'Kemi had organised a hen do for Suella a few years before,' reports one source. 'They were close. Kemi was a friend and admirer of Suella. She was really disappointed by what Suella did without consulting her.' Another source says:

There was huge disappointment that Suella couldn't come on board with Kemi. There was some thinking about that happening, but Suella went on *Peston* that night and said she was going to stand. She'd got her own backers, who encouraged her to do it. But it was a shame she did that. Kemi felt if Suella had come on board we could have had a different outcome. It was a mistake for Suella to do what she did.

By Friday 8 July, the day on which Badenoch formally declared that she would stand, it looked as though she would be one of at least eight candidates in the race. One parliamentary colleague, Nadine Dorries, tried to put her off by asking, 'Shouldn't you be running for Mayor of London instead?' Badenoch was furious at the slur but dismissed it as the desperate last gasp of an acolyte whose idol has fallen. Besides which, she was busy. With Rowley having agreed to act as her proposer and Lopez as her seconder, the next forty-eight hours were a whirlwind of activity as the trio tried to obtain the requisite twenty MPs to win a place on the first ballot while also recruiting a team of helpers, choosing a campaign logo, setting up a website, opening a campaign bank account and beginning a PR drive. Rowley's professional background as a project manager meant that it was natural for him to assume the role of chief organiser. 'It was wonderfully British, in a sense,' says Lopez.

> You'd never have had anything like this in American politics. It was an amateur campaign, in the very best sense of the word. On that Friday you were getting 'Ready for Rishi' tweets going out and Penny Mordaunt had her very slick video. But the contrast was useful in some respects. Kemi's approach was genuinely fresh and from the heart. And people responded to that.

The team based themselves at Rowley's house in Brixton. One early coup was a 700-word comment piece published in *The Times* on Saturday 9 July. Headlined 'I want to set us free by telling people the truth', Badenoch stated in it that 'people are exhausted by platitudes and empty rhetoric. Loving our country, our people or our party is not enough. What's missing is an intellectual grasp of what is required to run the country in an era of increased polarisation,

protectionism and populism amplified by social media.' Declaring
herself a Brexit voter, she wrote of her belief that Britain needed 'a
smart and nimble centre-right vision that can achieve things despite
entrenched opposition from a cultural establishment that will not
accept that the world has moved on from Blairism'. She advocated
lower taxes and tighter spending and set out her anti-woke stance
by declaring that government needed to be 'an effective and stream-
lined machine for delivery, not a piggy bank for pressure groups'.
The next day's *Sunday Telegraph* carried a long interview with her.
And on Monday 11 July, Michael Gove – whom Johnson had sacked
by telephone a few nights before – rowed in behind her, using a
piece in *The Sun* to praise her 'no bulls**t' approach to politics. 'If
you want to drive change, empower the right people,' Gove wrote.
'Kemi Badenoch has the Right Stuff.'

Gove's involvement in Badenoch's campaign was greeted with
high scepticism by some Tories, who thought he had decided to
push her forward in order to split the right of the party in favour of
a candidate more to his liking. One senior Tory MP says, 'Michael
Gove is a figure of suspicion who steams ahead with his own ideas.
Why did her back her? Either to spoil someone else's chances or
because he thought she might win then or later on and he would
emerge as the *éminence grise*.' Whatever the truth of Gove's ultimate
aim, he did not, of course, end up backing the winner. In any case,
on the day his article was published, Badenoch decided to honour
a commitment that had been in her diary for weeks by delivering
the main address at a cross-party free speech event organised by
peers and held in the House of Lords. Having reminded the 200
parliamentarians and campaigners who attended of her recent an
nouncement that all public buildings in England should have separate facilities for men and women, she revealed that civil servants

had tried to stop her from doing so. 'For those of you who saw my toilet announcement on the abolition of gender-neutral toilets, you wouldn't believe how tough it was to get that through,' she said. 'I had civil servants writing on the notice which I had put out saying that "you can't say that" and "we need to check whether that's something you are allowed to say".' When Badenoch explained that she had stood firm and 'didn't change a word', the audience applauded. She went on to warn that free speech was 'no longer something we can take for granted', adding:

> The reality is that attacks on free speech usually harm the people who have least power. I know from experience that speaking about subjects like race, ethnicity or LGBT rights can land you in hot water, but as an MP, I am safer than a lot of people who genuinely fear losing their job.

However heartfelt these sentiments were, the timing of the speech was undoubtedly useful.

By this point, Badenoch's team included Hudson Roe, who had been an adviser to a string of Cabinet ministers since 2017, and James Roberts, at that time the chief executive of the TaxPayers' Alliance. Another linchpin was Alex Morton, whom Badenoch had first encountered in 2006 when they both worked on Peter Lilley's foreign aid policy report. This connection did not mean that Lilley could be relied upon to back her, however. 'Alex got in touch with me and asked if I'd support Kemi,' remembers Lilley.

> I told him I thought she was terrific but I thought it was premature to be leader of the party since she'd never been a Cabinet minister. But in many ways I was better disposed to her than I

was any other candidate. I could see there was some point in her standing at that stage so that she became better known. But it wouldn't have been in her interests or the party's interests to get elected.

Nonetheless, Badenoch's team was confident that she had reached the magic number of twenty MPs. The leadership election process was approved by the 1922 Committee on 11 July and nominations opened and closed on 12 July, when Badenoch officially launched her campaign at the Policy Exchange think tank with a well-received twenty-minute speech introduced by Eddie Hughes MP. With her slogan 'Kemi for Prime Minister' on display, she spoke mainly about the economy and her determination to tackle divisive cultural issues. It did not go unnoticed that somebody had attached handwritten signs to the venue's gender-neutral lavatories, with one reading 'MEN' and the other 'LADIES'. There is no suggestion that Badenoch knew anything about this rogue behaviour, but she would have approved of the sentiment behind it. The left-wing journalist Julie Bindel was among those who backed Badenoch that morning, writing: 'I would rather give Donald Trump a massage than vote Tory, but if you want to know who I'd back to be the next PM? @KemiBadenoch all the way. She has her head screwed on. Only real grown up in the room.' According to Badenoch's friends, her stance on trans issues had already led to her forming many alliances with figures on the left which have endured.

At five o'clock the following afternoon, Sir Graham Brady, the chairman of the 1922 Committee, announced the results from the first ballot. Badenoch had secured forty votes and came fourth, making it through to the next round. Jeremy Hunt and Nadhim Zahawi were both eliminated. 'We used to watch the results in Julia's office,' remembers Rowley. 'Hamish would come, and we'd all gather there. The first round wildly exceeded ambitions and was at the very top of the range of our expectations. So we were extraordinarily excited. It was obvious there was something here that was resonating.'

That feeling was shared by the editor of *The Spectator*, Fraser Nelson.

The moment she stood, it electrified the debate, as far as I was concerned as an editor. I had to put out an order stopping pro-Kemi articles on the website. I didn't want it to seem that we were backing her. *The Spectator* is quite a laissez-faire place. We don't tell columnists what to think. It just happened that lots of them were mad for her. Almost every three hours there was another piece saying, 'She's great!' I had to limit it to no more than one pro-Kemi piece a day. The reason they all liked her was simple. She sees politics in all of its dimensions, including the cultural aspects. She talks about it effortlessly. She's seen now as an anti-woke warrior, but the irony is that for a long time she hadn't wanted to talk about it at all. A black woman talking about being black – she hates all that stuff. She initially hoped to stick to economics and avoid race completely. But it was clear that the Conservatives had in her an incredibly natural, passionate speaker. A lot of our writers are incredibly concerned about the cultural aspects of conservatism and they responded to it.

The second round of voting was held on Thursday 14 July. At that stage, Braverman was knocked out of the contest with twenty-seven votes – a loss of support, having received thirty-two votes in the first round. Badenoch again came fourth, this time with forty-nine votes. 'We were almost superstitious,' says Rowley.

We'd always watch in the same room. Each round, she built support. She got fifty-eight votes in the third round, when Tom Tugendhat was eliminated. We were happy she was still in the race, but we could see that unless something changed there was probably a natural end point to it. We were hoping that wasn't the case, but we sort of knew it was unlikely to go on. So we were prepared for it. And that was in the fourth round [on 19 July] when she went out having got fifty-nine votes.

It was noted that, unlike every other candidate who had dropped out before her, Badenoch did not endorse any of the remaining candidates – Penny Mordaunt, Rishi Sunak or Liz Truss. She and Mordaunt were not in line with one another ideologically. They had even crossed swords during one of the two televised leadership debates in which Badenoch appeared. Mordaunt had claimed that she was not in favour of gender self-identification and Badenoch had disputed this, provocatively yelling across the studio, 'Tell the truth, Liz!' when Truss was asked if Mordaunt's explanation was accurate. Truss dodged Badenoch's plea, though her evasiveness arguably spoke for itself.

Mordaunt was the next candidate to drop out, exiting the day after Badenoch. This meant that the final two MPs who would face the national members were Sunak and Truss. It is worth remembering that Badenoch had a unique perspective on their respective abilities, having had both of them as bosses simultaneously – Truss at the Government Equalities Office and Sunak at the Treasury. So whom did Badenoch back? The answer to this question involves, indirectly, Suella Braverman. 'Once Suella left the contest, she was one of the prime movers in installing Liz Truss, and that gave us no option but to back Liz,' says one Badenoch ally.

That was the problem. We had no choice but to vote for Liz. I've always quite liked Liz, but I've always had my concerns about her. Once Suella voted for Liz, you could see she'd win once she got to the members' stage. If we'd got Kemi to the members, versus Rishi Sunak, Kemi would have won and she wouldn't have blown everything up like Liz did. We'd have had a proper Conservative with a Conservative philosophy running the country.

There is no evidence that Badenoch indulged in this game of 'alternative history' herself, even if some of her supporters remain wistful about the outcome. In fact, she seems to have walked away from this political excursion feeling nothing but pleased about how things had gone. Without having had to try particularly hard, she had ultimately managed to attract the votes of almost one sixth of her party's MPs, she had made an impression on the millions of people who had followed the contest, and she had shown that she could articulate an argument rather than simply repeating a line she'd been given by her advisers. She had set out her stall as somebody who believed in border control, property ownership and the importance of the family – and as somebody who rejected cutting carbon emissions to zero by 2050. On that point, she had said with refreshing candour during the first TV debate:

The pledge was made in 2018 for 2050; none of us are going to be here as politicians in 2050. It's very easy to set a target you are not going to be responsible and accountable for when the time comes. The important thing is to make sure that we do this in a sustainable way. Many of the things we are doing could economically damage our country.

Interest in her political future was guaranteed, especially from Conservative Party members. Yet her closest allies are quick to say that she did not necessarily see it like this at all. 'It wasn't about an individual,' says Julia Lopez. 'It was about a group of people. Kemi's always said that. This is not some game. Nobody is ever the whole solution. This was about trying to shift how things were going in the country.'

Perhaps usefully, the short length of her involvement in the leadership battle – about two weeks – meant that very little money was spent on it, so she did not have to devote much time to fundraising or to declaring donations. She received £2,500 from an individual called Joanne Black and £10,000 from a company called Longrow Capital Ltd. No other funds or benefits were ever reported. Lee Rowley maintains that it was one of the most enjoyable political experiences of his career to date. 'It was such an unexpected adventure which none of us, three weeks before, had even considered we might be on,' he says.

> There was no big argument or crunching of gears. It just worked. Whether it would have worked for another two months is another question. But it just felt genuinely joyous to have the opportunity to talk about policy and philosophy and articulate something which was different and fresh. When it ended, everyone thought we'd achieved something. There was life in the party, interest in ideas.

Badenoch hadn't quite finished, however. Following the interim report of an independent review led by the senior NHS paediatrician Dr Hilary Cass, it was announced on 28 July that the NHS-funded Gender Identity Development Service at the Tavistock and Portman Foundation Trust in London would close. It was the only specialist gender identity clinic in Britain that catered for children up to the age of eighteen, but a growing number of questions about its services had been asked, notably by the BBC programme *Newsnight*. Badenoch wrote a revealing article in the *Sunday Times* in which she said that when she first became Equalities Minister in 2020, she had been forced to overrule civil servants in Whitehall who had tried to prevent her from speaking to a former Tavistock patient named Keira Bell, who had raised concerns about the clinic and then sued it. 'To my surprise, I was advised strongly and repeatedly by civil servants in the department that it would be "inappropriate" to speak to her,' she wrote. 'I overruled the advice. Along with other advisers across government I met Keira and listened to what she had to say. Her testimony was harrowing and brought many on the Zoom call to tears.' She insisted that not all civil servants were 'hostile' but went on: 'A small minority of activist officials are the tail wagging the dog, often to the dismay of their colleagues and the hand-wringing of far more senior officials.'

Sunak and Truss spent the rest of the summer on the road, touring the country as they sought to persuade Tory Party members of their fitness for the post of leader and, therefore, Prime Minister. Badenoch was able to spend several weeks with her family, safe in the knowledge that she had earned herself a role in the administration of whoever won. She was careful to stick to her line that she would not publicly back either of them, though as it appeared increasingly obvious that Truss was going to be the next premier, she did tell a *Daily Mail* podcast in mid-August, 'If you want somebody who's very maverick, I think Liz [would be the best option] ... I loved working with her because there was an unpredictability there that usually helped us get into the right place.' To some, these words were open to interpretation on several levels.

On 5 September, both of the remaining leadership candidates plus their teams and party officials gathered at the Queen Elizabeth II conference centre in Westminster to hear the result. Sunak had polled 60,399 votes, or 43 per cent; and Truss received the backing of 81,326 members, or 57 per cent of the vote. This victory was not as decisive as some had assumed it might be and the aura of precariousness around it did not take long to show itself in other ways. When Truss named her top team the next day, not a single Sunak supporter was invited to join it, an exclusionary policy which wiser heads believed would backfire. Badenoch was among those to be chosen, however. She was rewarded with her first Cabinet post. She had let it be known that she wanted to become Secretary of State for Education or Secretary of State for Culture, but she was instead appointed as Secretary of State for International Trade and President of the Board of Trade.

She had gone from being a backbencher to the front rank in the space of five years, a trajectory so swift it would have been almost unthinkable even in the recent past. She was also the only person who had not publicly backed Truss to be accorded the honour of a Cabinet post. Now she would have an opportunity to prove she could run a big government department, something she had never done before. At the top of the agenda was forging a trade deal with India, a diplomatic feat which the British government had already spent nine months working on to no avail. For reasons best known to Truss, though, the Equalities brief which had to a very large degree helped Badenoch to make her name politically was denied her. It didn't matter. By the following month, she would have it back again following a series of calamitous events which few could have foreseen and which nobody in Britain would ever wish to see repeated.

CHAPTER 10

MINISTER TO WATCH

Kemi Badenoch is not a morning person, according to those who know her well. One colleague goes so far as to say, 'She's not worth talking to before 9.30 a.m. and she hates the Westminster culture of breakfast meetings because she prefers to see her children before school.' With this in mind perhaps it wasn't surprising that her elevation to the top tier of British politics got off to an inauspicious start after she arrived twenty minutes late for her first Cabinet meeting, on 7 September. 'Does this mean the Indian trade deal will be delayed too?' one reporter shouted mischievously as she entered 10 Downing Street. She did not dignify this taunt with a response as she hurried inside to make her apologies to the new Prime Minister, but it must have dawned on her that the question was not entirely misplaced. The post she now occupied was one Liz Truss would be watching closely, having been the Secretary of State for International Trade herself for two years under Boris Johnson, putting Badenoch under a certain amount of pressure. Truss had enjoyed the job – particularly the globetrotting that was integral to it – though she has confessed that when she accepted it in 2019, she wept about the length of time she would have to spend away from her home and family. With three children aged nine, five and three, the same sense of dread must have passed over Badenoch – who is less of a keen traveller – in September 2022. It is known to have dawned on her husband, according to one friend, who says:

> I think Hamish found it a bit depressing to begin with. He realised there were implications to making the mother of young children International Trade Secretary. But they made it work. They always do. Hamish and she are like a team. He is an incredibly supportive political spouse. He makes sure things are OK at home so she can do what she has to do.

Truss had barely begun her duties when, on 8 September, the country was plunged into shock following the Queen's death. Ten days of mourning were declared, pausing politics and forcing a delay in the new administration's planned timetable of events. A state funeral was held on 19 September. The following day, government business resumed with a series of announcements. The most far-reaching of these, on 23 September, was made by the new Chancellor, Kwasi Kwarteng, in the Commons chamber. He called it the Growth Plan, but it soon became known as the mini-budget. It had four main planks: the cap on bankers' bonuses would be scrapped; plans to raise corporation tax from 19 per cent to 25 per cent would be abandoned; the basic rate of income tax would be cut by 1p; and the 45 per cent top rate of tax which kicked in at earnings of £150,000 would be abolished. Because Truss had already promised to freeze energy bills at an average of £2,500 per year for two years – a policy that would require borrowing between £120 billion and £150 billion – the markets were spooked. The question on many lips was: how could such vast loans, in conjunction with tax cuts, be sustained, particularly when no independent forecast by the Office for Budget Responsibility had been published? Within hours, sterling had sunk by 3.5 cents to reach its lowest level against the US dollar since 1985, closing at $1.09 and quickening pulses in Downing Street.

Badenoch was due to travel to New York two days later on her first overseas trip as part of an exercise to try to strengthen links between Britain and America. Her principal duties as International Trade Secretary were to attract investment, secure free trade agreements and try to reduce market access barriers for the benefit of British businesses and consumers. As somebody who had spoken in defence of Brexit, it made sense for her to fly the flag for British industry overseas in the post-Brexit world, but the markets' reaction to the mini-budget had made headlines globally, making her task all the harder. Some who worked alongside her had the feeling that matters were not helped by Truss's own activities. She had visited New York already that month and been forced to admit that a coveted trade deal with America could be years away, not least because of President Biden's perceived hostility towards Brexit. This left Badenoch with little to say that was new or positive.

There were other background tensions to negotiate too. 'Kemi and Liz had a difficult relationship,' remembers one colleague.

Liz viewed Kemi with suspicion. She thought she had to manage Kemi. And Kemi felt that, while Liz had sound ideological tendencies, she had always operated under Boris as though she was positioning herself. It was pretty awful when Liz appointed Kemi, because Liz never forgave her for not endorsing her publicly Kemi was the only person to get a Cabinet job who didn't endorse

Liz. Horrific briefings then appeared in the press. It was obvious they came from one of Liz's operatives and it was obvious which particular one. It was an active briefing war.

The first such story appeared two days after Kwarteng had delivered the mini-budget. It concerned Badenoch and Michael Gove, who had been spotted lunching together at Fortnum & Mason. Gove, who had supported Rishi Sunak for the leadership once Badenoch had been eliminated from that summer's contest, had been banished to the back benches by Truss, from where he was thought to be plotting and scheming. His rendezvous with Badenoch was taken as evidence of her somehow being complicit in a conspiracy. In the article, which appeared in the *Mail on Sunday*, he was labelled a 'snake' by an anonymous source while Badenoch was said to have insisted that her ministerial car should be driven by Gove's former government driver. The source told the newspaper: 'Michael is always up to something, he can't help himself. Kemi should not allow herself to become his puppet.' A source close to Badenoch believes that the motivation was clear. 'It was all about making sure there were no tall poppies around the Cabinet table. Her team didn't retaliate. Kemi hates blue-on-blue attacks.'

By the time Badenoch arrived at the fifth annual Atlantic Future Forum hosted on the HMS *Queen Elizabeth*, which was moored in New York, sterling's value had slipped below $1.07 (though it did quickly recover) and the International Monetary Fund had urged the British government to reappraise the terms of the mini-budget. This did not put her off her stride. 'Right now, there's a global growth slow-down underway,' she told attendees, who included figures from the defence and technology sector.

And if you'll forgive the pun, we need all hands on deck to get the world economy's wheels spinning again. And that's why in the UK we're going for growth in a big way. And in fact some of you may have heard some major reforms we announced on Friday to achieve this.

She boasted of Britain's low corporation tax rate, low-tax investment zones, infrastructure projects, increased spending on defence, and financial services reforms. 'There is radical change happening on our side of the Atlantic,' she went on. 'It's the kind of radical change that we've not seen for forty years.' During the 48-hour trip, she also met her American counterpart, Katherine Tai, plus representatives from the states of Oklahoma and South Carolina, with whom conversations took place about striking individual trade deals with those states, yet the prize of a formal US-wide agreement seemed just as elusive as it had been before she left London.

She returned to Britain in time for the Conservative Party conference, held that year in Birmingham. When it began, on Sunday 2 October, a sense of chaos reigned. UK government bonds were being sold off in a panic, pension funds were reportedly close to going bust and the mortgage markets were in turmoil. At the same time, a Cabinet row was brewing over Truss's intention to increase levels of immigration in order, she hoped, to boost economic growth. The *Sunday Times* named Badenoch, Business Secretary Jacob Rees-Mogg and Home Secretary Suella Braverman as three senior ministers who had raised questions about this idea. The newspaper also stated that Badenoch had been instructed by Truss to reach a free trade agreement with India by Diwali, which fell on 24 October. Badenoch was unhappy about this because of pressure to grant India a freedom of movement agreement as part of the deal, which would increase the number of visas Britain would have to issue to Indian nationals. Several hours after the story appeared, she was the guest of honour at a joint Institute of Economic Affairs/ TaxPayers' Alliance drinks reception where she made a speech in which she spoke fairly bluntly against Truss's proposition. 'Simply taking in numbers to boost GDP while GDP per capita falls is not the right way to do that,' she said. 'We need to look again at resolving our productivity issues and that means using capital better, not just getting cheaper and cheaper labour.'

In fact, Badenoch's apparent resistance to increased immigration was the least of Truss's worries. The next day, in a humiliating U-turn, Kwarteng's mini-budget plan to axe the top rate of tax was jettisoned. This move followed public criticism from Michael Gove, among others, leading to what was rapidly described as a Tory revolt against the policy. It was the first brick out of the Truss government's wall. By Thursday 20 October, it had collapsed into a heap of rubble when Truss announced after forty-four days that she was going to resign. Before this, Badenoch twice made public comments calling on colleagues to unite behind the embattled Prime Minister – once during a question-and-answer session with GB News at the Tory conference and again on 13 October during a visit to the Glenkinchie Distillery in East Lothian. Her pleas were ignored. The parliamentary party was torn. Indeed, the only point on which most of the warring factions seemed to agree was that Truss was out of her depth and would lead them to electoral disaster.

The 1922 Committee drew up new rules for an accelerated leadership contest. Candidates would need to show they had the backing of at least 100 MPs by 2 p.m. on Monday 24 October to proceed to the ballot. If necessary, the final two contenders would then take part in a televised hustings before party members had the final say in an online vote. The result would be announced by Friday 28 October. Just three months earlier, Badenoch had managed to secure fifty-nine supporters. If she did ever seriously contemplate running again that October, this aspiration did not last for long. To the amazement of many, Boris Johnson quickly made it clear that he was going to try to reclaim the crown which he felt he had been forced to surrender unjustly, potentially presenting an obstacle to her chances because some of her backers were Johnson loyalists. As it turned out, despite injecting some drama into the proceedings, Johnson's plan to reinstall himself in No. 10 ultimately came to nothing.

Penny Mordaunt was the first MP to announce her intention to stand, on Friday 21 October, but instead of following suit, Badenoch took to her desk to work on a 1,000-word opinion piece for the *Sunday Times* headlined 'Sunak is the serious, honest leader we need'. Dismissing the idea that the Conservative Party should be used as a vehicle to further the ambitions of any one individual, she wrote:

I have, on occasion, been a member of the Boris Johnson fan club. Even when I resigned from his government, I acknowledged his many strengths. He has been an asset to the country during some very difficult times. However, I am an even bigger fan of Margaret Thatcher, a formidable politician who did not duck difficult decisions, was extremely prudent and successfully carried out major reforms by winning the argument and taking the public with her. Mrs Thatcher won the public's trust and three elections in a row by making it about us, not about her. We need someone who can do the same. I believe that person is Rishi Sunak.

One friend was not surprised by the negative reference to Johnson.

> I remember going to a Saffron Walden constituency dinner held at the Cavalry and Guards Club in early 2019. Even back then – quite some time before she worked for Johnson – she was taken to task over what she thought of him. She said she wasn't a fan. She warned that he wasn't the right person to lead the party. And there was quite a nasty atmosphere because a lot of the people who were there really backed him.

Badenoch's piece appeared on the same day that Sunak issued a statement confirming his candidacy, and he welcomed her endorsement. She brought with her a block of votes that Sunak may not necessarily have needed but which Boris Johnson would have been reliant on, doubtless contributing to the former Prime Minister abandoning his scheme. Some detected the hand of Michael Gove in Badenoch's decision to back Sunak so publicly. Johnson himself was among them. Indeed, he eventually became so convinced of Gove's influence that somebody working on his behalf later let it be known that the knighthood that had been earmarked for Gove had been withdrawn.

By lunchtime on Monday 24 October, Sunak had secured the public backing of 193 MPs. Mordaunt's team claimed privately that she had ninety nominations, but two minutes before the 2 p.m. deadline, she issued a statement explaining that she was withdrawing from the contest. This left Sunak as the last candidate standing. Just as had happened to Michael Howard in 2003 and Theresa May in 2017, Sunak would become the leader of the Conservative Party by default following a 'coronation' and, as the leader of the largest party in Westminster, he also became Prime Minister. During his first forty-eight hours in Downing Street, he reshuffled the Cabinet that had been assembled by Truss in order, he hoped, that each wing of the parliamentary party might be better represented. It was announced that Badenoch would stay put as International Trade Secretary. She asked in addition to be given back the Equalities brief that Truss had removed from her seven weeks earlier. 'She'd worked well with Rishi at the Treasury,' says her special adviser Daniel El-Gamry. 'She always thought he was effective at chairing meetings. But she's not part of Rishi's inner circle. Rishi is not very cliquey.' However, another source, who is not necessarily well disposed towards Badenoch but who does have links to Sunak, believes that she was left where she was as part of a 'classic ruse to keep her out of the way because she would have to be overseas a lot'.

It was speedily made clear by Badenoch that the trade deal with India that Truss had wanted to secure so badly no longer faced a target date. When the Labour MP Kate Osamor suggested in the Commons chamber on 3 November that negotiations had stalled because of Home Secretary Suella Braverman's 'hardline opposition to migration', Badenoch was quick to kill off this theory. 'It is not true that negotiations with India have stalled, either because of the Home Secretary's comments or for any other reason,' she said. 'They are ongoing. What has changed is the deadline: as a result of my becoming Secretary of State, we are focusing on the deal and not the day, and that is the most important aspect.' A useful opportunity to relieve some pressure had been taken, yet this exchange highlighted just how difficult her job could be as she sought to balance competing interests both internationally and domestically. Many in Westminster considered her duties in this role to be among the most taxing in government. 'She had this very quick ascent to Cabinet and she genuinely focused on trying to get to grips with the job at

International Trade,' says one MP. 'There's a lot of travel. She spent a lot of time from October 2022 onwards just trying to understand stuff and she is primarily focused on her government jobs.'

Performing that balancing act was not the only challenge she faced, however. The scrutiny to which she had previously been subjected as Equalities Minister was also evident again. Just a few days later an edition of the BBC Radio 4 programme *Profile* was dedicated to her, but, having been broadcast, it had to be re-edited following complaints about inaccuracies. The *Daily Mail* reported that women's rights groups had criticised the programme for alleging that Badenoch was 'anti-trans'. This was in reference to the inclusion of what one source called a 'hostile activist journalist' called Ben Hunte. He had formerly worked as the BBC's LGBT correspondent before moving to the website Vice News, where in September 2021 he had written an article about an audio recording of Badenoch he had obtained in which she had supposedly 'mocked LGBTQ rights, questioned same-sex marriage, and called trans women "men"'. He was quoted in the *Profile* programme saying, 'There have been a number of situations over the past year that really do raise your eyebrows about what it means to be an Equalities Minister when you don't necessarily believe in all forms of equality within your portfolio.' Badenoch was well aware that this sort of criticism went with the territory she occupied and no doubt appreciated that others were prepared to leap to her defence, but friends say she is equipped with a gift that is rare among politicians: not minding. 'She just doesn't care what other people think of her,' says one ally.

Most of us wouldn't be able to absorb the level of hate that is directed at her thanks to the Equalities brief, but she is quite remarkable. For her, the hate is an affirmation of the rightness of her cause. She almost feeds off the hate. It's like a life-giving force.

Having put on her Trade Secretary hat again, her next stop was Washington DC, where she went in another attempt to promote UK–US trade. She gave a speech to the Cato Institute think tank, met Democrat and Republican politicians, addressed a US Chamber of Commerce event and spoke at the *Washington Post* Global Women's Summit. Even friends admit that it is hard to see how one person can combine two such contrasting government positions – one of which involves plenty of international travel – with constituency duties while also maintaining a family life. Yet having been elevated to the Cabinet, Badenoch was determined to cement her position as a serious player. One source who is familiar with her working patterns says:

> Her organisation could be better. Some people think there's a lack of structure and she needs to work on that. But on a personal level, people say she is easy to work with. She works hard, but weekends to her are sacrosanct for family, so people who work for her usually get weekends off too, when possible, though they may have to put in early mornings and late evenings during the week.

To assist her, she went on a recruitment drive in October 2022, though this again aroused suspicions that she was operating with Michael Gove's help. Word eventually got out that she had tried to hire as her Permanent Secretary in the Department for International Trade Sue Gray, the senior civil servant who had conducted the inquiry into the Partygate scandal which had proved to be Boris

Johnson's undoing. Gray had worked for Gove when he was the Chancellor of the Duchy of Lancaster and she came highly recommended by Badenoch's new principal private secretary (PPS), Ellie de la Bedoyere, who had also worked for Gove. 'Much to Kemi's displeasure, Simon Case, the Cabinet Secretary, said that Sue Gray couldn't be interviewed,' says one source. 'Case blocked it. That was probably done because there was so much bad blood thanks to Partygate. But Kemi was pleased to get Ellie as her PPS.' Ms de la Bedoyere was very close to Sue Gray, though she was later replaced by Annie Leigh, the niece of the Tory treasurer Lord Leigh.

In retrospect, some may feel it a shame that Badenoch didn't get her way, for Case's refusal to entertain Gray's transfer contributed to Gray quitting the civil service altogether to take a job as Sir Keir Starmer's chief of staff, enhancing his top team with her deep knowledge of Whitehall just as Labour consolidated its lead in the polls and, as a growing number of Tory MPs saw it, prepared for government. Gareth Davies was appointed as Permanent Secretary instead. Since taking up this job in January 2023, he is said to have been instrumental to Badenoch's operation. 'Kemi and Gareth have a great relationship,' says a Whitehall source. 'She appointed him. They have a routine weekly catch-up. He's created an infrastructure which allows her to be seen as a credible voice in business matters. He's made that possible. He's been very important.'

On her return to London from Washington, she attended the *Spectator* awards, where she was named 'Minister to Watch'. She used her acceptance speech to, seemingly, mock Boris Johnson's downfall, comparing him to the villain Thanos in the Avengers film series, from which she then quoted. 'I thought I might get resignation of the year, but actually it went to a far more deserving candidate,' she said. 'For those of you who are Marvel fans, it really was like *Avengers Assemble*. Sajid [Javid] was Captain America: "It's time to take down Thanos." We did it.' Some found it unsporting of her to jeer at Johnson, however gently, not least because she had benefited from him in career terms. Still, her dig against the former Prime Minister in 2022 didn't seem to matter, as the results of a survey conducted by the ConservativeHome website showed. It found that grassroots Tory activists regarded Ben Wallace, the Defence Secretary, as the clear favourite among party members with an approval rating of +83.2. In second place was Badenoch, whose rating was +63.4.

By this point, the Equalities brief was occupying increasing amounts of Badenoch's time and thought. In late November, she fielded questions in the Commons chamber from her own side and from the Labour Party about so-called conversion therapy, the practice of trying to alter a person's sexual orientation or gender identity. Successive Conservative governments since the days of Theresa May had promised to introduce legislation to ban such treatments, but it had not materialised. Badenoch told MPs the delay was attributable to the issue being 'not as simple as members opposite would like it to be'. She added: 'This is a very, very complex area and when we do it, we're going to do it right and permanently.' In fact, she is known to have been instinctively wary of the proposed ban, fearful that parents and guardians could end up being treated as criminals merely for advising children about matters relating to sexuality or gender. At the time of writing, the ban had not found its way into law and appeared to have been kicked into touch, to the delight of many Tory MPs.

Another political headache hit a few days later when politicians in Scotland were preparing to vote on the Gender Recognition Bill (Scotland). Under the existing UK-wide law, adults wanting to legally change their sex had to apply for a gender recognition certificate, be medically diagnosed with gender dysphoria and live full-time under their acquired gender for at least two years. The Scottish legislation, which was first introduced in the Scottish Parliament in March 2022, would give everybody aged sixteen and over the ability to change their sex without receiving a medical diagnosis, meaning they would be able to apply for a birth certificate featuring their new sex and receive it within six months. Badenoch is said to have been alive to the potential risks of this proposal. She was not alone in worrying that it could have the consequence of giving biological males a licence to access female-only spaces such as changing rooms and lavatories, or allow biologically male Scottish prisoners in English jails to request a transfer to a women's prison. There were even suggestions that it could lead to 'trans tourism', whereby a transgender woman could legally speed up changing their gender by going through the process in Scotland and then use their new status to access women-only spaces in England and Wales, where different rules applied. Badenoch was the first MP to act on her doubts by seeking legal advice about its implications for the rest of the UK. In an attempt to halt the legislation, she wrote to Nicola Sturgeon, the Scottish First Minister, in early December, saying that she was 'concerned' that the proposals would create a 'divergence' of approach on a 'complex and important issue' and warning that the application of different rules in Scotland could harm the Equality Act. Her voice was considered pivotal in the ensuing debate.

Soon afterwards, she travelled to India to begin a sixth round of negotiations of the free trade agreement which had by then been under discussion for the best part of a year. Despite her and India's commerce minister, Piyush Goyal, insisting that both sides remained committed to the plan, no announcement came from their meeting, though they maintained that progress had been made. Shortly after she arrived back in London, the Gender Recognition Bill was passed by the Scottish Parliament. The Westminster government mulled what to do over Christmas, and in January 2023 Rishi Sunak announced that the legislation would be blocked under Section 35 of the Scotland Act 1998. Sunak was the first Prime Minister to take advantage of this power since the Scottish Parliament's creation in 1999. Although it was left to the Secretary of State for Scotland, Alister Jack, to draw up the Section 35 order, and in many ways to claim the credit for the move, Badenoch's active involvement did not remain entirely behind the scenes. She was invited by the Equalities Committee at Holyrood 'to give further clarity' on the government's decision to intervene in this piece of Scottish legislation, but she declined. The decision to veto the Gender Recognition Bill took on greater significance later that month when a sex criminal called Isla Bryson, who was convicted of raping two women when named Adam Graham, was sent initially to a women's prison in Scotland. The ensuing controversy about the Gender Recognition Bill was linked by some commentators to Sturgeon's sudden resignation in February 2023.

For Badenoch personally, the situation gave her a further opportunity to demonstrate her refusal to buckle under the weight of what some considered groupthink. When the SNP politician Kate Forbes, who was in contention to replace Sturgeon, voiced her opposition to same-sex marriage because it clashed with her Christian beliefs, Badenoch defended Forbes's right to be true to herself. 'I support same-sex marriage and like anyone I'm disappointed when anyone disagrees with me,' she explained to the website Politico.

But if you're asking me to condemn someone for their religious views, you've failed to understand the basic responsibilities of being Minister for Equality. I actually admire [Forbes] for not being dishonest. It'd be very easy for her to tell lies, just so that she could win that election, and she's not doing that, and I think that that's something that people need to take into account.

In her international trade role, she showed that she was equally prepared to challenge the status quo. In January 2023, she travelled to the Swiss ski resort of Davos to attend the World Economic Forum. Despite her personal professional limitations as somebody who had never run a business, she spoke frankly about what she discovered there. Having spent several days in meetings with company executives and politicians, she made clear that the gathering itself was nothing to be sceptical of but that the vocally anti-Brexit Confederation of British Industry, Britain's biggest business lobby group, certainly was. 'The CBI was talking down the UK to business,' she told *The Times* on her return.

I didn't find that very helpful. You wouldn't find a French business association saying, 'Things are very difficult, people are unhappy.' It doesn't mean that behind closed doors, we don't have frank conversations. It doesn't mean that we're not aware of issues or we're not taking them seriously. But when you go to an investment conference that's about investment I think we all need to be on Team UK. Everybody [else] was there advertising their country.

The commitment she had shown to her new responsibilities was rewarded on 7 February 2023 when she was promoted in a government reshuffle to the newly created post of Secretary of State for Business and Trade. She was now in charge of a bigger department and would have a more prominent role in the government.

Indeed, the promotion meant that she now had, in effect, three jobs – Equalities Minister, Business Secretary and International Trade Secretary – if not three salaries. Some questioned the wisdom of this arrangement. What message did it send about how seriously the government took each brief if only one person was responsible for all three of them?

Badenoch is said to have calculated quickly that she should try to split her duties so that three quarters of her time was spent on her Business and Trade roles and the other quarter on being the Equalities Minister, though she soon found that the latter took up a disproportionate amount of her time. 'She has a weekly meeting for about ninety minutes with Marcus Bell, the most senior civil servant who works on equalities policy, and a select few others,' explains one colleague.

> He presents all the advice to her that needs her clearance. The civil servants who work on equalities are based in the Department for Education building, so she has to find a way of making sure they aren't forgotten. She also brought in external people to help as well like Mercy Muroki and Nikki Da Costa. She didn't do this on the Business side because that department is so well resourced. For about an hour each day private secretaries will present advice to her on business and trade matters. That's how she divides the process. It's tough. She has more work than Liz Truss had because Liz didn't also have the Business portfolio.

Badenoch's ministerial red boxes are apparently tackled verbally and she prefers to use a computer tablet instead of a ministerial folder. 'She doesn't ask for a printout where she makes written comments and submissions every day.'

Within forty-eight hours of being appointed to her expanded role, she made what some considered her first blunder as a Cabinet minister. She was in Italy to sign a new 'trade partnership' that did little in practice but was apparently designed to improve trade links between the two countries. Giving an interview to Sky News while she was in Rome, she was asked whether the UK 'come what may, would always need to have a steel industry'. To this she answered, 'Nothing is ever a given.' This phrase came back to haunt her two weeks later when it was announced that the Chinese-owned firm British Steel was to close the coking ovens at its Scunthorpe works – among the last such facilities in Britain – with the loss of 260 jobs. The two chief reasons for this were high energy costs and the need to invest in expensive environmentally friendly technologies. Alex Brummer in the *Daily Mail* accused Badenoch of showing 'worrying naivety' in her choice of words as he pointed out the importance to the nation of being able to produce the highest-grade steel for Britain's defence and nuclear industries – especially during the war in Ukraine – and the need for the Tory Party to preserve jobs in Red Wall seats.

Brummer further wondered if she had failed her first test as Business Secretary. The Labour Party was also predictably outraged at her apparent indifference to British industry and workers. At the time of writing, government talks regarding a £600 million taxpayer-funded support package for the Scunthorpe works continued, as British Steel tried to raise £1.25 billion for its decarbonisation plans. Incidentally, a few months after saying, 'Nothing is ever a given,' Badenoch also oversaw a £500 million commitment to keep Britain's largest steelworks at Port Talbot open so that steel could be produced more cleanly there but with the loss of about 2,500 jobs. With layoffs this size as a consequence of green energy, some queried what had happened to her rejection of cutting net carbon emissions to zero by 2050, a point of view that had earned her much praise in some quarters during the leadership contest in 2022. 'Many of the things we are doing could economically damage our country,' she had said at the time. Had she been captured by the Whitehall establishment?

And yet in other settings she was unafraid to show the independent spirit that had helped her make it to the fourth round of the leadership contest. When she gave evidence to the House of Commons Equalities Committee on 1 March, Labour MP Carolyn Harris asked her whether the menopause could become a protected characteristic under the Equalities Act. Badenoch barely concealed her sarcasm. 'We have so many things that people ask for protected characteristics: carers, single people, having ginger hair,' she said. 'Creating a special character of menopause is a misunderstanding of what protected characteristics are. They are immutable characteristics. We have nine that cover everyone. The menopause can be dealt with alongside three existing ones – age, sex and disability – because it is a health condition.' The committee chairwoman Caroline Nokes – a Conservative MP on the left of the party and to whom Badenoch is not close – then asked what she thought about only fourteen FTSE 100 companies voluntarily reporting ethnicity pay gap data. A similarly no-nonsense reply followed. 'I do not think it is for me to tell businesses what they should do,' Badenoch said. 'That is one of the reasons I think it should be voluntary. Ethnicity pay gap reporting is very different from gender pay gap reporting.' She added:

It is easy for people to say they are doing ethnicity pay gap reporting, and what they are doing is junk. Then they will put out data talking about how inclusive they are, when what they are doing is nothing of the sort ... I speak as someone who has worked in the corporate sector and has seen lots of junk initiatives being promoted that are meant to pacify ethnic minorities in the workplace.

A Labour MP named Kim Johnson received a similarly hard-headed response when she asked what Badenoch thought about a recent visit to Britain made by a UN working group which had concluded that 'from the perspective of people of African descent, racism in the UK is structural, institutional, and systematic'. Badenoch rubbished their words. 'We strongly reject most of their findings in that area,' she said.

I actually found the way that the working group viewed African people as a homogenous group to be slightly disturbing. It was a very superficial analysis. I am almost certain they had written the report before they had come here, and they just wanted to confirm what they felt about the UK ... The fact is that every single country they visited, they found to be racist, and all those countries happen to be Western countries. They do not go where there are actually serious problems.

Would, say, a white male MP have been able to say any of this so bluntly?

Of course, her detractors were not limited to MPs on select committees. They also operated less openly, tipping off newspapers about her perceived shortcomings. For example, the following week's *Mail on Sunday* reported that she had refused Rishi Sunak's request to go with him and several other Cabinet ministers to Paris to attend a summit with French President Emmanuel Macron at which she was to have stood in for the Chancellor, Jeremy Hunt, at a meeting with Emmanuel Moulin, the director general of the French Treasury. She apparently told Downing Street that she had 'business to attend to' in her constituency. This prompted somebody who was familiar with the situation to suggest that Badenoch was getting 'too big for her boots', as they claimed, 'It is impossible to get her to do anything we ask. She just says no.' Once again, it was suggested that she was being 'manipulated' by Michael Gove, her supposed puppet master. It was also claimed that Liz Truss thought her 'rude' and had tried to avoid talking to her during her tenure as Prime Minister. A source close to Badenoch fought back, explaining that she had been in Israel for most of the week.

> Kemi is not just the most senior black woman in government – she is the only black woman in government and in the Tory Party. What a shame that just after International Women's Day there are people trying to say the Business Secretary is getting too big for her boots, yet mysteriously at the same time doesn't know her own mind and is someone else's puppet.

Another source claims that the reason Badenoch refused to go to Paris was because of her promise to attend an event for Essex farmers. 'I remember Minette Batters of the NFU wrote to her saying how grateful she was that she had honoured the commitment,' says this person.

As Jeremy Hunt prepared for his first spring budget as Chancellor later that month, Badenoch relayed to him companies' concerns about his planned rise in corporation tax from 19 per cent to 25 per cent. Her representations fell on deaf ears, but a plan to tax sovereign wealth funds investing in Britain was dropped by Hunt, partly in response to her expressing fears that this could force Middle Eastern investors to withdraw from infrastructure and commercial property projects. By late March, it was being reported that during her first 200 days in Cabinet, at least £2.2 billion of foreign trade barriers which had prevented British businesses from selling goods and services had been dismantled. The good news was crowned when Britain's application to join the Comprehensive and Progressive Agreement for Trans-Pacific Partnership (CPTPP) was formally accepted a few days later. This trade deal, which would cut tariffs for UK exporters on some goods to eleven countries including Japan, Canada, Australia and Mexico, had been two years in the making. It was begun by the first ever International Trade Secretary Dr Liam Fox, who then passed the baton to his eventual successor, Liz Truss. She saw in it a way of taking on the economic might of China. But it was finished off by Badenoch. She is said to have formed a personal relationship with the ambassador of every CPTPP country as part of a charm offensive when the long-running dispute between the UK and the EU over the installation of a 'hard' border between Northern Ireland and the Republic of Ireland threatened Britain's invitation to become a CPTPP member. This was Britain's biggest trade deal since the vote to leave the EU seven years earlier and was held up as the epitome of the 'Brexit bonus' of which those who had campaigned to leave the EU had always dreamed. Being able, as an independent nation, to tap into a market of 500 million people with £12 trillion of income was the type of boost Britain needed.

Yet, according to some doubters, becoming a CPTPP member meant that it would be impossible for Britain to rejoin the EU, a point of view that threatened to reopen old wounds. The BBC also claimed on its website that Britain's membership of this trans-pacific club might add only 0.08 per cent to the economy over the following ten years. As a rule, Badenoch does not like giving live broadcast interviews, believing they are now a kind of 'gotcha' journalism designed principally to wrongfoot politicians, but she was happy to oblige on this occasion. Speaking on Radio 4's *Today* programme just a few hours after finalising the late-night deal over a Zoom call, she rubbished these numbers when they were put to her, saying she believed they had originated from a 'scoping assessment' carried out by civil servants in 2021 which was itself based on data from 2014. She followed this up with an article for the *Daily Mail* to explain that the CPTPP's share of the world economy was in line to exceed the EU's in future and she criticised the BBC for its assertion that the deal amounted to little.

The CPTPP agreement was scheduled to be ratified by the second half of 2024 at the latest, but with opinion polls by now suggesting the Conservatives were going to be voted out of office at the next general election, the only question was whether it would come into force while Badenoch was still the Business and Trade Secretary, or whether a minister in a future Labour government would steer it into port instead. As somebody who was increasingly being talked about as a future Tory leader, this mattered to Badenoch more than most.

CHAPTER 11

CONSOLIDATION

When Ron DeSantis, the conservative Republican Governor of Florida, visited London in late April 2023, he had hoped to secure a meeting with Rishi Sunak. Officially, Sunak made clear that this would not be possible because he had a prior engagement. Unofficially, the Prime Minister knew that any such appointment might upset Donald Trump, who, like DeSantis, wanted to run for the White House in the next US election. Appearing to take sides by welcoming DeSantis into 10 Downing Street would be unwise. As a Cabinet minister, Kemi Badenoch faced no such dilemma. She was happy to set aside some time for the American. They met at the Lloyd's building in the City, where they discussed the rise of progressive 'woke' ideology, agreeing that it had to a large degree been exported to Britain from the United States and praising each other's efforts to combat it. Afterwards, a tweet went out to DeSantis's 2 million Twitter followers saying, 'Today @GovRonDeSantis met with @KemiBadenoch, who has been branded by British media as the "Anti-woke darling of the right" (a badge of honor!) Two great conservative fighters on [a] mission.' The eye-catching publicity continued forty-eight hours later when the *Sunday Times* published the result of a poll asking, 'Is Kemi Badenoch a future Prime Minister?' Of the 13,418 votes cast, 51 per cent answered 'Yes' while 49 per cent said 'No'. Public opinion on her may have been evenly split, according to the newspaper's findings, but here was more proof that she was well on the way to achieving what most politicians crave: public recognition.

A damaging episode soon followed, however. By early May 2023, it was strongly rumoured that the Retained EU Law Bill – a piece of legislation conceived during Boris Johnson's premiership, endorsed by Sunak and subsequently voted for by a majority of MPs – was to be diluted. Because this bill had been designed to rid the statute book of about 4,000 EU regulations in one go, it was considered by Brexiteers to be of great symbolic significance, quite apart from having some practical benefits. Yet its so-called sunset clause, under which every law made in Brussels would expire automatically at the end of 2023, was to be abandoned after the concerns of businesses, civil servants and members of the House of Lords had all been heard. The upshot was that only 600 regulations would be junked. Johnson's government had promised a 'Brexit bonfire' of EU laws. Under Sunak's administration, Tory Brexiteers believed it would resemble something closer to a campfire. They felt a deep sense of betrayal. 'The government didn't believe in it,' explains one MP who was close to events. 'Sunak has never had a Eurosceptic Cabinet. The new regime inherited this bill, but they didn't believe in it and that's why it was watered down.' It fell to Badenoch, as Business and Trade Secretary, to oversee the reversal. The fact that she seems to have put several Tory noses out of joint as she did so only made a bad situation worse and, at the time of writing, she had not been forgiven by certain members of her party.

First, she held a private meeting with a clutch of Eurosceptic Tory

MPs from the European Research Group (ERG) during which it was confirmed that the weakening process was indeed going to take place. She followed this up with a written ministerial statement and an article in the *Daily Telegraph*, published on 10 May, in which she set out the reasons for the change of heart. The next day she was forced to appear in the Commons chamber after an urgent question was tabled by her Tory colleague Bill Cash, a key ERG figure and the chairman of the European Scrutiny Committee, which assesses the legal and political importance of draft EU legislation. This was when things went wrong.

As the session began, the Speaker, Sir Lindsay Hoyle, said it was 'highly regrettable' that the government had gone against protocol by not first making an oral statement on the matter but had instead used a newspaper article to make its case. Badenoch replied, 'I am very sorry, Mr Speaker, that the sequencing that we chose was not to your satisfaction.' However regretful she had intended to sound when she uttered these words, her tone seemed to come across as plain sarcastic. Hoyle interrupted her, appalled. 'Who do you think you are speaking to, Secretary of State?' he demanded. Badenoch apologised. When Bill Cash then pointed out that she had been asked three times since February to appear before the European Scrutiny Committee and asked why she hadn't done so, she was again thought to have sounded impudent as she prefaced her answer by saying, 'I think he knows that he has heard the answers before...' Then another Tory MP, David Jones, followed up Cash's contribution. 'Given the seriousness of the volte-face she has now performed, will she accept the invitation of the chairman [Cash], made this morning, and appear before the committee next week? If not, why not?' Badenoch said breezily, 'Because I am in Switzerland next week and in the Middle East the week after. As I said to the chair of the European Scrutiny Committee, I am happy to appear in front of the committee, and now that we have a settled policy I will do so.'

A third Tory MP, Mark Francois, also took her to task, as he pointed out that in January the bill had passed its third reading without any Tory MPs voting against it. 'Why, after going to the House of Lords, has the government performed a massive climbdown on their own bill, despite having such strong support from their own backbenchers? Secretary of State, what on earth are you playing at?' Francois implored. 'He should know that I am not somebody who gets pushed around lightly,' Badenoch answered.

> The fact is that I went in, looked at the detail and decided that this was the best way to deliver this. I stress again that this was not the Prime Minister's decision. As a Secretary of State, I have to be responsible and look at what we can make sure is deliverable. This is the best way to get [Francois] what he wants.

During the 45-minute sitting, awkward comments were not restricted to Conservative MPs. Labour's spokesman, Justin Madders, called the U-turn a 'shambles'. And when SNP MP Carol Monaghan rose to her feet, she first made a point of referring to Badenoch's 'wonderfully patronising manner, which she has used many times this morning'.

There is no doubt that the events that culminated in her 'patronising' performance in the chamber on 11 May have had a lasting impact on Badenoch's reputation as far as one group in the parliamentary party is concerned. To her credit, she twice made clear to MPs that she accepted responsibility for the decision, which she said was hers alone rather than Sunak's. Her view was that slowing down the process of scrapping the laws in order to work out exactly which ones were being jettisoned was preferable to leaving their fate to civil servants. She did, however, goad her own benches when she said, 'It is delightful to see those on the Labour front bench and the ERG on the same side for once, as they claim to be. If I am upsetting people on both sides, I am probably taking the pragmatic middle ground and I am pleased to be doing so.' Experienced parliamentarians doubted that this was a sensible way to speak to her colleagues. If nothing else, they assumed she must have known that Eurosceptics feared the decision to keep thousands of EU laws would leave the door open to Britain binding itself to the EU again one day.

At this time, questions about the future of Sunak's leadership were growing. In the previous week's local elections, the Tories had lost 1,063 seats, while Labour had gained 537 and the Liberal Democrats 407. A strand of Tory MPs, including Sir John Redwood, concluded openly that Badenoch's credentials as a potential leader had been dented beyond repair because of her handling of the matter. Others, speaking anonymously, accused her at the time of being 'lazy and condescending'. It did not go unnoticed that she was not invited to the NatCon conference in Westminster in mid-May, a three-day gathering of international right-wing politicians which had grown in significance since being launched in 2016. Other senior Tories, including Jacob Rees-Mogg and Lord Frost, were down to speak there. So was Suella Braverman, the Home Secretary, who was seen by some as having leap-frogged Badenoch in the affections of the right wing of the parliamentary party. Some maintain that ill-feeling towards Badenoch has not abated since. 'Her relationship with the Eurosceptic right died in the Commons chamber that day,' says one MP. 'She's a Eurosceptic in name only.' Grassroots party members expressed their disapproval as well. A ConservativeHome poll found that her net satisfaction score had dropped by almost 15 points, from 60.4 to 46.7, pushing her from second to fourth place in the popularity stakes behind Ben Wallace, Penny Mordaunt – who had attracted a significant amount of attention at the coronation of King Charles III that month as the bearer of the Sword of State – and James Cleverly.

On 6 June, at the sixth time of asking, Badenoch did appear before the European Scrutiny Committee. There, she and David Jones locked horns again, as she explained to him:

> What we want to do is get rid of laws we don't need and there is a process for that. It is not the bonfire of regulations. We are not arsonists. I am certainly not an arsonist. I am a Conservative. I don't think a bonfire of regulations is what we wanted. What we wanted was the reform and removal of things we did not need.

Jones asked if she thought her approach was 'disrespectful to the House of Commons', but she seemed to go on the attack.

> Something you are not saying, we had private meetings, David, we had private meetings where we discussed this extensively, because I knew you had concerns. And it is public knowledge we had private meetings, because when I thought I was having private and confidential meetings I was reading the contents in the *Daily Telegraph*.

Jones was stung by this episode and Badenoch's friends say this is reflective of her overall approach. 'It could be described as a short-coming of hers,' says one. 'Off duty she is easy company and fun to be with, but when it comes to politics she takes no prisoners, whoever she is dealing with.' As for the Retained EU Law (Revo-cation and Reform) Act 2023, it made it onto the statute book the following month, though Bill Cash wrote to Sunak and Badenoch telling them that he believed the laws that were being scrapped re-lated to matters that were 'trivial, obsolete and are not legally and/or politically important'. Even if hardline Eurosceptics would never be happy with the way Brexit had been handled, there is little evidence that Badenoch felt the need to try to accommodate them.

By the summer of 2023, Rishi Sunak had been in Downing Street for nine months and readers of Tory-supporting newspapers had become well used to a diet of stories that promised the party would be annihilated at the next general election. Many of Boris Johnson's followers dreamed of his return to the front line, but his resignation as an MP in early June put paid to this idea. He was swiftly followed in quitting the Commons by his close friend Nigel Adams. In an unconnected resignation, another Tory MP, David Warburton, an-nounced his departure, triggering three by-elections that were held on 20 July. These contests served mainly to emphasise the fractured state of the parliamentary party and it was taken as surprising when one of the seats – ironically, Uxbridge and South Ruislip, where Johnson had been the MP – was held. Even Tory supporters had assumed all three would be lost and lobby journalists were only too happy to lavish attention on the party's difficulties.

Following the defeats, and with Johnson's close ally Nadine Dor-ries having declared her intention to stand down (though without confirming when she would formally resign her seat in the Com-mons), the volume of anti-Tory press speculation seemed to inten-sify. Some articles pushed the interests of Suella Braverman. Others were designed to amplify Badenoch's putative leadership ambi-tions. Yet it was not obvious whether each MP's supporters were responsible for placing them or whether they were the products of a rival faction which was agitating for its own, as yet unclear, reasons.

An example of this came in late July, when the *Mail on Sunday* reported that Badenoch had been invited to a meeting of the No Turning Back group, whose membership consists of pro-Thatcherite MPs. She reportedly told those gathered that she, like them, believed that the government was not doing enough to capitalise on post-Brexit freedoms, saying, 'I'm with you, I'm one of you.' An ally of hers dismissed claims that she was recruiting backers for a potential leadership bid, insisting she would 'rather be Business Secretary in a Conservative government' than Leader of the Opposition, but a Tory MP told the newspaper, 'Kemi sees herself as one of the few grown-ups who can take over from Rishi and realign the party to the right. They're on manoeuvres and potential allies are being spoken to in those terms.' The following week, the same newspaper returned to this theme, pointing out that the website backingbadenoch.co.uk, which was set up in 2022, had been updated. Badenoch's office explained that she had nothing to do with the website, which was apparently overseen by grassroots campaigners. The message those who spoke for her wanted to convey was that she favoured the status quo. Even if this was true, however, assumptions that a portion of the party wanted Sunak to be replaced before the next general election – which had to be held by January 2025 – only deepened. And even if Sunak managed to hold on until then, who would succeed him in the event of a defeat? Everything Badenoch said and did from then on would be seen through this prism, whether she liked it or not.

A notable battle that she fought that summer as Business Secretary concerned delaying the 2030 deadline for outlawing the sale of new petrol and diesel cars. Under revised plans, the ban was postponed by five years, to 2035. When Sunak announced this in late September, Badenoch let it be known that she had lobbied him and the Chancellor, Jeremy Hunt, over the issue, making clear her belief that no environmental goal, however noble, was immune to practical considerations such as cost. She was uncompromising. When LBC asked what she thought about Lord Goldsmith's criticism of the delay, she said:

> Zac Goldsmith is someone who cares very much about the environment, he is a friend of mine. But the fact is he has way more money than pretty much everyone in the UK. This is not how we make decisions. We need to make decisions based on what the facts are.

And when Jayne Secker, an interviewer on Sky News, put it to Badenoch that the policy wouldn't help the poorest in society because they don't drive cars, she was given even shorter shrift. 'That is a ludicrous statement,' Badenoch scolded. 'If you step outside of London, come to my constituency, you will find the poorest in society drive because they live in a rural area … What you've said is actually quite astonishing … We need to think about everybody, not just the metropolitan bubble.'

She was also credited that summer with helping to end a controversial aspect of the relationship between the government and Stonewall. The charity had taken to publishing an annual list of Britain's top 100 employers known as the Diversity Champions Programme, which it called the 'gold standard for LGBTQ inclusion'. In 2020, three ministries including the Home Office were included on the chart, but the 2023 list contained none. This was said to be because in August of that year Badenoch had instructed every government department that had not done so already to withdraw from the scheme owing to its adherence to gender self-identification, among other things. Many in her own party were delighted that she was able to exert such influence. 'She's very clear that sexuality and gender are completely different things,' says the gay Tory MP Conor Burns. 'That annoys the provisional wing of the LGBT movement known as Stonewall, who are bullies in corporate Britain. She's standing up to them and they cannot cope with it.'

On the eve of the Tory conference in Manchester that October, an interview she gave to the *Sunday Times* was perceived by some as an opportunity to apply pressure on Sunak over the key matter of Britain's membership of the European Convention on Human Rights (ECHR), which many felt was being abused by lawyers acting for illegal immigrants, and to remind voters that her nearest rival, Suella Braverman, did not have a monopoly on this subject. Just a few days earlier, Braverman had attracted attention by making a speech in Washington in which she said that if the ECHR continued to get in the way of the government rolling out its policy of flying illegal immigrants from Britain to Rwanda, quitting the organisation could not be ruled out. Echoing these comments, Badenoch told the *Sunday Times*, 'It's certainly not racist to talk about reviewing conventions which we joined 100 years ago. I think that's a ridiculous argument.' (In fact, the ECHR was conceived in 1950.) She went on to say:

People present this argument as being something that's very extreme, but ... even in legal circles, a point that they make is that this convention needs updating. We should be able to have an honest conversation [about it]. That debate has not happened yet and I think it is right that the Home Secretary is trying to start one.

It was striking that two potential Tory leaders, both of whom had discussed their own immigrant status in the past, were now seen by some observers to be trying to outdo each other on the vexed question of illegal immigration. As for net migration figures, which the Office for National Statistics estimated at 745,000 for the year 2022, Badenoch made clear when asked that she thought that number too high. She pinned the blame on Boris Johnson's post-Brexit visa system.

Inevitably, Badenoch's wide-ranging conference speech the next day – her first since 2017, when she had introduced Theresa May – was taken as a further leadership pitch. She mentioned Nigel Lawson, Margaret Thatcher, Thomas Sowell and Martin Luther King as she set out her stall. She spoke of her pride at being the Business and Trade Secretary and her sadness when she thought about her political opponents 'and their friends in the media' who 'continue to speak about our country like it's an irrelevant nation'. As she acknowledged the difficulties of being in government anywhere in the world, she went on: 'It is only when I am back in the UK that I am told that all these issues are down to Brexit. Our political opponents are obsessed with viewing every problem as Brexit, relentlessly talking down our country.' She ticked off a string of Business and Trade achievements such as the £600 million invested by BMW in Oxfordshire, the £4 billion investment in a new gigafactory in Somerset and the CPTPP partnership, and urged everyone to contrast these successes with Keir Starmer's policies. 'His answer to the global challenges we face is to tax more, regulate more and ask the EU what to do next.' She heaped praise on Sunak, saying:

We have in Rishi Sunak a Prime Minister who is making decisions for the long term interest of our country, even when he gets flak for it … He has the intellect and work ethic to steer us through whatever comes next, to tell the country what it needs to hear, not just what it wants to hear.

She criticised those who would 're-racialise' society. The loudest cheers were reserved for her mentions of the Labour Party 'bending the knee' at an 'altar of intolerance'. She then attacked Labour for wanting young people to believe in

a narrative of hopelessness that says there is no point in trying, because British society is against you and you're better off asking for reparations. A narrative that tells children like mine that the odds are stacked against them. I tell my children this is the best country in the world to be black – because it's a country that sees people, not labels.

And she rounded off by paying tribute to the various groups that fought against the gender self-ID policy, saying, 'The left accuses us of fighting a culture war. But we will not apologise for fighting for common sense. I will not apologise for fighting for a society that knows what a woman is.'

The following morning's splash in the *Daily Mail* – 'Britain Is The Best Country To Be Black In, Says Kemi' – acted as proof not only that she had struck the right tone but also that she had won over a key media player. By contrast, coverage of Suella Braverman's speech was not accorded the same prominence. Arguably, it was just as powerful, but it was seen as unashamedly – perhaps deliberately – controversial, as she predicted that a 'hurricane' of mass migration was coming to Britain and branded the Human Rights Act the 'Criminal Rights Act'. Speaking at an event hosted by Fraser

Nelson a few hours after Braverman's effort, Badenoch was cautious in her own comments on immigration, saying, 'We live in a multi-racial society … But we have to be very careful about how we explain and express immigration policies, so that people aren't getting echoes of things that are less palatable.' Was this the subtle dig at her rival that some took it as? When Nelson asked her about her own aims, she again emphasised the importance of supporting Sunak. 'It is a problem, because it makes people think you are not a team player … when actually the complete opposite is true,' she said. She pointed out that the 'unbelievably clever' Prime Minister had faced the same hurdle when he was the Chancellor and she urged everybody to put self-obsession to one side. 'Labour are coming for us,' she warned. 'We need to stop messing around and get focused on winning the next election.' Inevitably, however, whatever she said, many observers continued to believe that she was carefully plotting her own course to the leadership. Reflecting the high regard in which some Tory activists hold Badenoch, one audience member even shouted out at this point, 'We want *you*, Kemi!'

Another fan who showed her appreciation for Badenoch that month was Lady Falkner, the chair of the Equality and Human Rights Commission (EHRC), which is responsible for promoting and enforcing equality laws in England, Scotland and Wales. Falkner, a former Liberal Democrat candidate who was appointed in 2020, had been placed under official investigation by the EHRC in February 2023 for alleged bullying, discrimination and harassment of staff at the taxpayer-funded organisation, forcing her into the unenviable position of having to find £30,000 to cover her own legal advice. In July 2023, Badenoch, in her capacity as Equalities Minister, intervened by ordering an independent legal review into the EHRC's handling of the complaints it had received. This review recommended in late October 2023 that the EHRC's investigation be closed forthwith, thereby clearing Falkner of any wrongdoing. It transpired that the original complaints against Falkner had been motivated in part by her recommending changes to the Equality Act that would protect biological women by guaranteeing that specific female-only spaces would be off-limits to trans women, angering some EHRC staff. Yet Badenoch had supported Falkner throughout, not least by refusing to accept her resignation at the beginning of the hugely bruising process. Such fights are said to affect Badenoch deeply as well. One ally says:

> Of the three government jobs Kemi does, the Equalities brief takes up a disproportionate amount of time. This is because of its constant nature. She has to fight the machinery of government, the activists, the broadcast media and others pretty much all the time. It is a constant battle. But she is determined to do it. I would say she finds it the most fulfilling of the three jobs she does.

A few days later, Badenoch spoke at the Alliance for Responsible Citizenship, a gathering in London for conservative thinkers from across the world who were concerned about division and fragmentation in Western society. It was also addressed by the Tory MPs Danny Kruger, Miriam Cates and the SNP politician Kate Forbes, the Canadian psychologist Jordan Peterson, the US House of Representatives Speaker Mike Johnson and the author Tom Holland. This was a valuable opportunity for Badenoch to press her case in a centre-right setting and she did so by linking her various government posts as she lambasted the way of the world, pointing out that the fixation on identity was harming the West's economic prospects.

'I don't think that things are as bad as others do, but I do think we are on the cusp,' she said.

> There is an inflexion point coming and we need to be very focused … and that means not being distracted by all sorts of silly things like pronouns and what critical race theory is saying and measuring people's skin colour and so on. Whenever I see too much invested in those sorts of things it means that companies and individuals are not dealing with their core purposes and that is why I am sceptical about so many of those things.

She added:

> Something weird is happening, and that is that in a low-growth environment, businesses are now competing not on who can make the most profit but who can signal the most virtue and hope that is a way of generating investment. You see that manifest itself in things like ESG [environment, social and governance investing] that's not actually doing ESG, and DEI [diversity, equity and inclusion] that's not actually doing DEI.

Another speaker at the Alliance for Responsible Citizenship conference was Michael Gove. Soon afterwards, two curious stories concerning him and Badenoch were published which warrant acknowledgement. The first appeared in Nadine Dorries's book *The Plot: The Political Assassination of Boris Johnson*. Described as a behind-the-scenes account of the machinations of the Tory Party, the book stated that ever since the premiership of David Cameron, a clique that includes a Tory adviser called Dougie

Smith has determined the identity of party leaders. One of Smith's chief selling points seems to be that very little about him is known publicly, other than that he is in his sixties, he is married to Boris Johnson's former adviser Munira Mirza, he is fiercely averse to 'woke' culture and he joined the Tory Party payroll in 2002. His official duties are understood to have included identifying candidates. Dorries's book claimed that Smith, who has worked in the political office at 10 Downing Street, was – or had been – operating in cahoots with Gove and that after a mere twelve months in office it had been decided that Sunak would be replaced by Badenoch. Dorries's book quoted a source as saying Gove had been 'building up Kemi Badenoch as the next leader of the Conservative Party, because that was part of the plan and it still is. He's been mentoring Kemi for a long time, possibly, originally, at Dougie's behest.' It should be said that Dorries described Badenoch as 'rude' in her book and that neither she nor Johnson have had any time for her since she quit the government and stood for the leadership in July 2022. Was this simply Dorries's attempt at sabotaging Badenoch's chances of one day leading the party?

The predictable chatter inspired by the book may have had something to do with the second story concerning Badenoch. It appeared in *The Times* on 11 November, immediately after Dorries's book was serialised in the *Daily Mail*. Headlined 'Cabinet rift after Gove's affair with married acquaintance of Badenoch', it was fairly light on detail other than to explain that Gove had had a dalliance with the unnamed 'acquaintance' and that this betrayal had caused a 'significant deterioration' in relations between him and Badenoch. In fact, Badenoch only knew the woman in question because she and her husband had attended Cambridge University with Hamish Badenoch. When the extramarital relationship with Gove was exposed, they divorced. Quite apart from nobody knowing how Gove was caught, two other questions that have perplexed many in Westminster are how and why this information came to light at all. For obvious reasons, it seems highly unlikely that Gove planted it in *The Times*. And the unnamed woman and her former husband – who are both private individuals – are also known to have been keen to avoid publicity, not least to spare their children any heartache.

Whoever was responsible for alerting the press about the affair, and whatever their motive, it did have a benefit to Badenoch insofar as it put some distance between her and Gove. His assumed status as her 'puppet master' had overshadowed her own assumed objectives until this point. Even though her friends had always dismissed this idea – and many of them point out that Gove has drifted leftwards over his political career while Badenoch considers herself to be on the right – publication of the story represented an opportunity to dispel the persistent idea that she was controlled by him. It would be distinctly curious if Badenoch herself had had anything to do with briefing *The Times*, however. Friends say that while she gets on with several newspaper and magazine editors, she 'has a problem' with lobby journalists. 'She loves to read the ConservativeHome website and *The Spectator*,' reports one ally. 'But she likes honesty. It's a big thing for her.' The clear inference is that she believes much of what is written by those who work in the lobby can be dismissed as invention, tittle-tattle or gossip and she prefers to write her own articles when she has something to say. As for Gove, Badenoch insists that they have had a functioning professional relationship since she found out about his affair, but nothing more.

The Times was the venue for another political development during the same week, and one that was far more consequential. After several weeks of demonstrations and protests in central London about the Israel–Hamas war, Suella Braverman wrote a piece that was published in the newspaper on 9 November in which she claimed there was 'a perception that senior police officers play favourites when it comes to protesters' and were tougher on right-wing extremists than pro-Palestinian 'mobs'. It soon became known that Downing Street had asked her to tone down her language but she had ignored the request, leading to her dismissal as Home Secretary on 13 November. This was the prelude to a wider Cabinet reshuffle in which David Cameron – having been given a peerage – made a surprise return to government as Foreign Secretary. Badenoch's position was unaffected by these events, which, it was reported at the time, may have disappointed her because she would have accepted Braverman's post had it been offered. By contrast, most people concluded that Braverman had got the result she wanted. Bookmakers had by this point decided that the chance of a Labour government emerging after the next election was at 92 per cent and opinion polls had recorded Labour's lead consistently at 20 points. It was said that by orchestrating her own sacking, Braverman had positioned herself as Sunak's eventual successor if the party opted for a candidate from the right wing of the party next time there was a leadership contest. The thinking went that she would use the remaining time before a general election to boost her standing as a credible alternative to Sunak and, indeed, to Badenoch or anybody else who aspired to be leader.

As theories about the future leadership of the Tory Party went, this one was considered more plausible than that which had been pushed by Nadine Dorries. One MP friend of Badenoch takes the idea seriously and observes, 'Kemi and Suella are perfectly friendly and they have a lot in common, but they don't get on. Suella is waiting to be leader but she doesn't have the political skills of someone like Nigel Farage. She's allowed herself to be portrayed as divisive. Kemi is more thoughtful.' Another friend is blunter, saying, 'I think Kemi's view of Suella's time in the Home Office was that she'd talked a lot but delivered very little.'

In any case, Badenoch had other fish to fry. A day after the excitement in Westminster caused by Braverman, she was in Florida to sign a trade pact with her admirer Ron DeSantis. This was the seventh UK–US state level memorandum of understanding and, like the previous six, it was designed to increase trade and investment by making it quicker and easier for British firms to do business in these particular American states, which had a combined GDP of £3.3 trillion. The next day, Badenoch travelled to San Francisco for a CPTPP meeting. Having signed off Britain's membership of the trade bloc in July, she could boast of Britain becoming the first new country and the only European nation that had been accepted as a member since its formation in 2018 (though formal membership would not be in place until late 2024). By late 2023, its members accounted for 16 per cent of the global economy – the same as the 27-nation European Union. The World Bank calculated that by 2050, CPTPP's existing members would generate about 25 per cent of global GDP while the EU's share would shrink to 10 per cent over the same period. These were achievements that would, Badenoch believed, bear fruit in the future. She told the *Sunday Telegraph*:

If Florida was a country, it would be the fifteenth-biggest economy in the world, the same size as Spain. The Biden administration has shut the door on new free trade agreements with all countries – we won't see a US–UK free trade deal any time soon – so instead, we're using our Brexit freedom to sign state deals, staying nimble and agile, removing barriers reducing trade.

Soon afterwards, she opened talks with South Korea about strengthening trade ties.

In early December, Badenoch gave a statement to the Commons announcing changes to the list of countries from which Britain would accept gender recognition certificates. The subsequent debate turned to the as-yet unresolved matter of what guidance the government could offer to schools when it came to supporting pupils who questioned their gender. This led to some lively exchanges during which Badenoch set out her fears for children who were in this position. 'We are seeing, I would say, almost an epidemic of young gay children being told that they are trans and being put on a medical pathway for irreversible decisions, and they are regretting it,' she cautioned. She said that primary school children should be banned from socially transitioning 'except in the most extreme safeguarding cases – and I expect that to include clinical advice'. She added that when it came to self-identification, 'Stonewall does not decide the law in this country'.

A small number of Labour MPs including Ben Bradshaw and Chris Bryant challenged her, with Bryant saying, 'As a gay man, I feel less safe today than I did three years or five years ago. Why? Sometimes it is because of the rhetoric used in the public debate, including by the minister.' It was left to the lesbian rights activist Julie Bindel to defend Badenoch, which she did in a powerful piece in the *Daily Telegraph* praising her honesty. 'Listening to Badenoch yesterday was a breath of fresh air for this lifelong Labour voter, who could never envisage voting Tory,' Bindel stated.

> I support Badenoch 100 per cent in her endeavours to expose this ideology for what it is … Some women have lost their jobs, reputations, and even been arrested for saying the things

Badenoch said in Parliament yesterday – yet she simply made common-sense, fact-based statements … What Badenoch did was the most progressive thing I have seen in Parliament for a long time. The Labour Party should hang its head in shame, and Badenoch should be awarded a medal.

A week later, Badenoch gave evidence to the Commons Women and Equalities Select Committee, which provided further insights into the difficulties of her job but also the sheer certainty of her views on the subject of transgender identity. During a tense ninety-second exchange, Labour MP Kate Osborne accused her of making 'statements using inflammatory language that likens children and young people coming out as trans to the spread of disease'. This, presumably, was a reference to her use the previous week of the word 'epidemic'. Badenoch was appalled. 'I've never said that,' she exclaimed. 'That is a lie and I think you should withdraw that statement. That is a lie. You are lying.' Osborne, stunned, denied that she was lying and the committee chairwoman Caroline Nokes, whose own progressive views have not escaped the attention of journalists, stepped in to upbraid Badenoch for using 'unparliamentary language'. But when Badenoch – index finger jabbing – asked Osborne to pinpoint when and where she had allegedly spoken in the manner suggested, Osborne was unable to produce the evidence. Badenoch verbally pummelled her once more for good measure. 'I will not have my name maligned by people making false statements about me,' she said. 'We have to do better than this.'

Her parliamentary colleague Lee Rowley MP, who is gay, is convinced that Badenoch has been typecast as a difficult, homophobic woman, but in his eyes nothing could be further from the truth. 'There's no doubt Kemi is direct. We need directness in politics right now – there is so much that needs to be done. But what I find bizarre is the really outlandish claims about her having certain phobias, whispers of evangelical Christianity or not liking gay people. It's just fundamentally wrong and lazy by people who think that because she doesn't agree with everything they say, it must come from a certain viewpoint,' Rowley says.

> Kemi, like me, is a child of the 1990s. She grew up in a period of social change. We are relaxed with the vast majority of it. We have a completely live-and-let-live attitude so long as it doesn't affect others. What happened was that after the good reforms which equalised things – gay marriage, pension rights, more tolerance and so on – some activists decided they wanted more. And polite society decided they don't know how to handle that. So they indulge it. The trans stuff, some of the racial activism – it overshot massively. Now everyone gets to have their own version of the truth. Now we see that the earlier positive moves to give people equality of opportunity are instead being twisted into anti-meritocratic, tick-box exercises, which is dividing society. Those people started a culture war by pushing way beyond what reasonable people – whatever their race, sexuality, background – think and what common sense says. We just want to let people get on with their lives.

Plain-talking performances such as the one she put in at the Equality Committee hearing ensured that by the end of 2023 Badenoch continued to be spoken of as a future Tory leader – possibly even as Sunak's direct replacement. A week before Christmas, the government finally published trans guidance for schools which said teachers in England should only let pupils identify as the opposite gender in rare cases after consultation with their parents. This was met with strong opposition. The charity Stonewall called it 'actively dangerous' and the aforementioned Kate Osborne MP described it as 'cruel and unworkable' and advised teachers to ignore it.

Badenoch countered these views in the *Daily Mail*. 'Children have been led to believe that they can be born in the wrong body and that we have an abstract "gender identity" which is separate to our biological sex,' she wrote. 'This is a contested and confused ideology.'

Few in Westminster were surprised when readers of ConservativeHome voted Badenoch the Minister of the Year for 2023. And with a general election almost guaranteed to take place in 2024, she was happy to accept the accolade.

CHAPTER 12

KILLING BAD IDEAS

Over the first four days of 2024, ITV broadcast a miscarriage of justice drama which, on paper, sounded somewhat esoteric but which turned out to be hugely popular and highly consequential. The programme, *Mr Bates vs The Post Office*, told the true story of hundreds of sub-postmasters who were wrongly prosecuted for fraud, theft and false accounting because of a rogue computer system called Horizon. Some went to jail and others were left financially ruined. At least four are known to have died by suicide. Despite wrecking so many lives over a period of more than fifteen years, and although a statutory inquiry into the matter was launched in 2021, the scandal was not widely known until ITV's series was shown. Its effect was immediate. Less than a week after the final episode had aired, more than 1 million people had signed a petition demanding justice for the sub-postmasters, and Rishi Sunak told MPs during Prime Minister's Questions on 10 January that he was going to introduce new legislation that would exonerate and compensate them. This unusual situation placed the ongoing story at the centre of the nation's consciousness, and Kemi Badenoch, whose department ultimately had oversight of the state-owned Post

Office, was soon dragged into it. The manner in which she handled the situation once again said much about her uncompromising approach to politics, even if not everybody was impressed.

The Horizon IT system was developed by the Japanese technology firm Fujitsu and by the middle of January Badenoch had written to its chief executive, Takahito Tokita, seeking a discussion about securing a compensation package for the sub-postmasters, but in fact Badenoch was no stranger to this scandal. She was unusual among Cabinet members in having grasped its scale before it became a cause célèbre, mentioning it in her speech to the Tory conference three months earlier:

> We are on the side of those whose voices have been ignored for too long. Sometimes it feels like the system is against you. Sometimes the system gets it wrong. That happened with the Post Office Horizon scandal. Scores of postmasters across Britain were wrongly convicted due to faulty software. Hard-working men and women endured unimaginable hardship, financial ruin, jail time. I was determined to right this wrong. No amount of money can fully compensate for liberty unjustly taken away. But with the help of my Business Minister Kevin Hollinrake, last month we announced that every wrongfully convicted postmaster will receive £600,000 in compensation. Telling the truth is the most important thing in politics. It's the only way to really show whose side we're on.

Then, on 27 January, it was announced that Henry Staunton, the 75-year-old chairman of the Post Office, had agreed to resign after receiving a phone call from Badenoch in which he was effectively sacked. Contemporary reports quoted Badenoch as saying, 'The

Post Office is rightfully under a heightened level of scrutiny at this time. With that in mind, I felt there was a need for new leadership, and we have parted ways with mutual consent.'

Under normal circumstances, Staunton's dismissal might have been noticed by fewer people in Britain, but thanks to ITV's drama it attracted considerable attention. Three weeks later, on 18 February, the *Sunday Times* published an interview with Staunton, who had previously run WH Smith and had been at the Post Office for barely a year. In it, he maintained that he was told by a senior civil servant in Badenoch's department – before ITV's drama was broadcast – to stall compensation payments to sub-postmasters so that the government could 'limp into the election' with a smaller financial liability. He also claimed that when Badenoch had sacked him, she had said to him, 'Well, someone's got to take the rap for this.'

Characteristically, Badenoch did not take these accusations on the chin. She posted a lengthy defence on Twitter in which she suggested Staunton was a liar, that whistleblowers had made assertions about his conduct and that his interview was a 'disgraceful misrepresentation' of her conversation with him. She added:

Far from 'taking the rap', I dismissed Staunton due to very serious allegations about his conduct while chair of the Post Office, including blocking an investigation into that conduct. My department is responsible for whistleblowers and I wouldn't ignore the allegations. My call with Staunton was with officials. They took a complete record. He has given an interview full of lies about our conversation during his dismissal. The details will emerge soon enough as I won't let the matter rest here, but will be discussing with government lawyers. Henry Staunton had a lack of grip getting justice for postmasters. The serious concerns over his conduct were the reasons I asked him to step down. That he chose to run to the media with made-up anecdotes and a series of falsehoods confirms I made the correct decision. We will make a statement tomorrow telling the truth about what's been happening.

There was some nervousness among colleagues the next afternoon when she rose to address the Commons. Could the hitherto re-spected Staunton be telling the truth? As it happened, Badenoch stepped up her attack. She declared that Staunton had a 'cavalier attitude to governance' and said his *Sunday Times* interview was 'a blatant attempt to seek revenge' following his dismissal. She re-vealed that he had been under formal investigation 'into allegations made regarding his conduct, including serious matters such as bullying' and suggested there had been concerns about his 'willing-ness to cooperate' with that investigation. 'I dismissed him because there were serious concerns about his behaviour as chair, including those raised by other directors on the board,' she said, adding that 'to suggest otherwise, for whatever personal motives, is a disgrace'. In the interests of transparency, she explained that officials from her department were on the line during the phone call in which she dis-missed Staunton and that minutes from that call would be placed in the Commons library so that MPs and the public 'can see the truth'.

The Labour Party thought this was a spat that could be capital-ised on and at Prime Minister's Questions two days later, Sir Keir Starmer asked Rishi Sunak whether he would repeat Badenoch's allegation that Staunton was lying over claims he was told to 'go slow' on compensation for sub-postmasters. Sunak swerved in his first answer, so Starmer tried again, but there was no major change in Sunak's response. By then, the Prime Minister presumably knew of a letter written by Sarah Munby, the former Permanent

Secretary to the Department for Business, which denied Staunton's claim about the compensation payments and provided supporting documents which Munby said proved the inaccuracy of Staunton's claims. Munby's letter, which was published that day, added that the funding that had been discussed related to operational funding, not compensation funding.

Starmer wasn't the only one to go for Badenoch during that session of PMQs. The Labour MP Ben Bradshaw took to his feet a few minutes later to challenge her on a different front, telling Sunak that although, in her capacity as Minister for Women and Equalities, she had recently told the House that she had engaged 'extensively' with LGBT organisations since her appointment eighteen months ago, she had not met a single LGBT organisation. He then said, 'But [she] has met two fringe groups that actively campaign against transgender rights.' He went on: 'What is the problem that the Prime Minister and a section of his party have with trans people, and that his Minister has with the truth?' Sunak spoke in her defence, saying that 'it is completely reasonable to highlight the importance of biological sex' when it comes to questions of gender and identity. 'Nobody should be stigmatised or demonised for pointing out that fact,' he added.

It didn't end there. After PMQs, Badenoch came in for further scrutiny in the chamber when the shadow leader of the Commons, Lucy Powell, sought – via a point of order – further clarification on the wrangle with Staunton. Then another Labour MP, Liam Byrne, used the same mechanism to question Badenoch's recent claim that trade talks with Canada had 'not broken down' when, he said, the Canadian high commissioner, Ralph Goodale, had apparently contradicted this. 'How do we get to the bottom of whether these trade talks are going on in the Secretary of State's mind or happening in real life?' Byrne asked provocatively. This was beginning to resemble a concerted effort from Labour to target Badenoch just when she appeared to be under strain. The row later became more complicated as it also engulfed the Post Office's chief executive, Nick Read, but in April 2024 a line was drawn under it as far as Badenoch was concerned when an investigation carried out by Marianne Tutin, an employment barrister at Devereux Chambers, assessed fourteen allegations about the conduct of Read and Staunton. Ultimately, Read was cleared of all wrongdoing, but Tutin upheld one allegation against Staunton and said that his conduct during the investigation gave her 'cause for concern' about the 'reliability and integrity of their evidence'.

Staunton later said that he had 'serious questions' about the process, but in the final analysis, Badenoch emerged unscathed from the skirmish, professionally speaking. Some in her party wondered if she had behaved appropriately. Had she gone too far on Twitter? Would anybody want to succeed Staunton as Post Office chairman if there was a risk they might one day end up having a very public argument with the Business Secretary? An unnamed former minister told the *Mail on Sunday*, 'How she behaved with Staunton is how she behaves with everyone. She crosses the road to start a fight.' Yet one well-placed source insists that Badenoch's attitude to the Post Office scandal is driven by her desire for the truth. 'She cottoned on to the seriousness of this long before any other MP,' says this person. 'Many people are unaware of her work behind the scenes in trying to correct this problem. She deserves credit for her efforts.'

Throughout this period, pressure had again been building on Sunak, as speculation about his prospects of leading the Conservatives into the next election nagged. In mid-January, the *Daily Telegraph* published the results of an anonymously funded poll conducted by YouGov which predicted that the party was on course to retain only 169 seats at the general election against Labour's projected 385 seats. 'Tories facing 1997-style general election wipeout' the front-page headline roared. Accompanying analysis from the Conservative peer Lord Frost made clear that Sunak having inherited an unruly party in 2022 may not have been his fault, but it was his problem. Frost warned that unless the Prime Minister got to grips with issues such as the cost of net zero and high immigration, the party would be reduced to a pile of 'smoking rubble'.

At the time the poll was published, Sunak was preparing to push through legislation relating to the Rwanda Bill, the Tories' flagship policy which said that any asylum seeker entering the UK illegally from a safe country such as France could be sent to Rwanda to have their claim processed there, rather than in Britain. It was a hugely problematic plan. Labour opposed it and many Tory MPs were sceptical of it – either feeling it was too weak or too tough, depending on which wing of the party they were from. There was a fear that enough members of the so-called 'five families' inside the parliamentary party – each representing a faction on the right – could rebel and bring Sunak down in the process. Perhaps the only thing preventing a quick defenestration was that nobody could agree on who should replace him.

Amid the maelstrom, *The Times* reported that Badenoch had warned Sunak's chief of staff, Liam Booth-Smith, in December 2023 that the Rwanda legislation should be toughened up in order to prevent immigrants from lodging individual appeals against their deportation. A source told the newspaper, 'Kemi was aware that the Prime Minister faced a serious rebellion and he had to try and accommodate them, so she went in to see Liam. She was trying to avoid the rebel MPs turning against the government.' Having taken advice from Victoria Prentis, the Attorney General, Sunak had apparently rejected Badenoch's suggestion on the grounds that it would put Britain in breach of international law. Since Badenoch's meeting with Booth-Smith had been private, and because nothing had come of it, some wondered why details of their conversation were gracing the pages of a national newspaper at all. Had somebody from Badenoch's team planted the story in order to present her as a sensible, uniting team player? Had the paper been tipped off by a supporter who wished to see her replace Sunak? Or had Downing Street leaked the news in order to wrong-foot Badenoch? It was certainly considered noteworthy when the well-connected commentator Andrew Marr disclosed he had been told by a Commons source that Badenoch had been worried the government might lose the vote on the bill's third reading on 17 January because 'she didn't want a premature leadership contest or early general election'. Marr added, 'She was overheard observing that "Rishi has got to own the defeat"'.

Sunak's political future appeared to rest on whether the bill would pass. In fact, the government did not lose the vote and, after a protracted battle between the Commons and the Lords, the bill completed its passage through Parliament on 22 April. Between mid-January and that date, however, questions about Badenoch's leadership hopes continued. In late January, for example, she was asked on Sky's *Sunday Morning with Trevor Phillips* programme about the apparent desire of some Tory MPs to install her as leader. She hit back with force, saying that Sunak had her 'full support'. She went on: 'Quite frankly, the people who keep putting my name in there are not my friends. They don't care about me. They don't care about my family or what this would entail. They are just stirring.' She blamed the rumours on a small number of agitating MPs, adding,

'We can't just keep treating Prime Ministers as if they are disposable. "Oh, the polls aren't doing so well, so let's toss someone else and find another person" – that's quite wrong.' One close political ally is convinced that this is a fair representation of Badenoch's true position. 'Kemi and Rishi have a cordial, professional relationship,' they say.

> She obviously wants him to do well. She wants him to do the best he can. She's constructive. Personally, they get on fine. There is a difference of political philosophy and of world view. She set out her view during the leadership contest in 2022, and we don't have that [with Sunak]. But we want the party to succeed and continue. There's a huge respect for the party and the person who leads it. That institutional respect comes first.

In early February, a wide-ranging interview with her appeared in *The Times*, complete with a photo shoot at the house she rents in her constituency, in which voters were invited to find out a little more about her. The 4,000-word piece, written by Janice Turner, pitched her as 'the woman tipped to be the next Tory leader', though in fact it concentrated less on politics and more on her as a person. Some sceptics in the party who had heard her defend Sunak a few days earlier wondered what the purpose of this article was if it wasn't a public relations exercise preparing the ground for a future leadership bid.

A good portion of the interview picked over her views on race, beginning with her opinion that it is a mistake to conflate those who have come to Britain from Africa with those whose roots are in the Caribbean. 'Until recently, Africans came here from middle-class homes to go to university and, if we stayed around, we worked in banks,' Badenoch pointed out. 'Whereas the Windrush generation came to do working-class jobs: driving buses, nursing.' She said she had experienced racism 'very rarely' and talked about the work of the social scientist Remi Adekoya, who, according to Janice Turner, 'found children raised in families where misfortunes were always blamed on racism tend to see discrimination everywhere'. She also spoke out against mixed-race children such as her own being regarded as black. 'This is the "one-drop rule": white is the pure thing and any other ancestry takes you out of that category,' Badenoch said.

> Context is important: in Nigeria my children would be oyinbo, which means white. Yet here I see a lot of mixed-race people who seem embarrassed about the white side of their family. Kehinde Andrews has written a book called *The Psychosis of Whiteness*. This man is mixed race! I think if you're mixed race, you should have the best of both worlds.

Turner also covered Badenoch's views on gender, writing that

> the policy area in which she has won respect across the political spectrum, including from left-wing feminists, is her handling of the gender debate. While Rishi Sunak makes crude culture war points such as, 'A man is a man and a woman is a woman,' Badenoch has immersed herself in this arcane and contentious issue.

Badenoch said she had become involved in the debate because 'I feel being a woman is a much stronger part of my identity than being black or Nigerian. Because it is so real. Bringing a child into the world grounds you in the reality of being a woman. Puberty, menstruation, menopause. It is very biological.' She was then asked if she thought that Caroline Nokes, the chairwoman of the Equalities Select Committee, was trying to undermine her. Badenoch's answer was careful. 'I think there are some questions where it's not really scrutinising policy. It's about the person. And I'm on top of my brief. I will not be tripped up,' she said. Less than a week after the interview was published, she travelled to Nigeria to sign a trade deal that would apply across sectors including legal and financial services, education and energy. Having left the country twenty-eight years earlier, it must have struck her as remarkable that she was returning as a British Cabinet minister.

Two days later, on 15 February, came a pair of by-elections which generated more bad news for Sunak. The first, at Kingswood, was caused by the resignation of the Tory MP Chris Skidmore, who quit the Commons in protest at the government's decision to issue more oil and gas licences. He was replaced by Labour's Damien Egan. The second, at Wellingborough, had been a Conservative seat until October 2023 when the sitting MP, Peter Bone, lost the whip. Following a recall petition, Bone was replaced by a Labour candidate, Gen Kitchen. The following week, the Tory MP Lee Anderson had the whip suspended after he refused to apologise for saying during a discussion on GB News that 'Islamists' had 'got control' of the Mayor of London, Sadiq Khan, and 'they've got control of London … He's actually given our capital city away to his mates.' On 11 March, Anderson defected to the Reform Party, becoming its only MP in the House of Commons.

As if that wasn't enough for Sunak to contend with, that same day *The Guardian* reported that the biggest ever individual donor to the Tory Party, Frank Hester, who had given £10 million over a period of months, had once made offensive remarks during a private meeting attended by employees of his software company, the Phoenix Partnership. Hester was reported to have said in 2019: 'It's like trying not to be racist, but you see Diane Abbott on the TV and you're just like … you just want to hate all black women because she's there, and I don't hate all black women at all, but I think she should be shot.' Somewhat ironically, Abbott, who was first elected as a Labour MP in 1987, had had the whip suspended in April 2023 after she wrote a letter to *The Observer* in which she had downplayed suggestions of racism against Jewish people. Now, public outrage was directed at Downing Street for failing to condemn Hester. After twenty-four hours of what was taken to be dithering, Badenoch filled the vacuum, as she took to Twitter to label Hester's comments 'racist'. She was the first Cabinet minister to use this term to describe this important Tory Party figure, breaking ranks with Sunak in the process. 'Hester's 2019 comments, as reported, were racist,' Badenoch wrote.

> I welcome his apology. Abbott and I disagree on a lot. But the idea of linking criticism of her to being a black woman is appalling. It's never acceptable to conflate someone's views with the colour of their skin. MPs have a difficult job balancing multiple interests – often under threats of intimidation as we saw recently in parliament. Some people make flippant comments without thinking of this context. This is why there needs to be space for forgiveness where there is contrition.

She later said that the party should not return Hester's donations.

However strongly felt her opinion was, it had the immediate effect of putting Sunak on the spot. One commentator described her Twitter post as a 'grenade'. Within hours, the Prime Minister had been forced to follow her lead. Was this part of a wider plan on Badenoch's part to position herself as a leader-in-waiting? It is true that by this point there was – once again – talk of a plot to oust Sunak, but the name on the lips of those who were said to be agitating was Penny Mordaunt, not Kemi Badenoch. With that said, a possible subplot in this particular storyline had it that Mordaunt was in fact being used by the right as a stalking horse so that in the event of a leadership contest, they could field their preferred candidate, though that individual's name never emerged.

In any case, on 13 March, the day after her tweet about Hester was sent, it was another Abbott who occupied Badenoch's thoughts – Greg Abbott, the Governor of Texas. They met in Downing Street to sign a trade deal designed to benefit the energy, life sciences and professional services sectors. The following week, a report into the equality, diversity and inclusion (EDI) industry commissioned by Badenoch was published. It cited research suggesting that Britain had almost twice as many diversity and inclusion workers per 10,000 employees as any other country, with 10,000 in the private sector alone at a cost of £557 million annually. The report stated that while employers had a duty to 'fully grasp and apply the law', it was not the job of companies to have a 'sophisticated knowledge of the demographic, historical and socio-economic debates relating to the relative advantage and disadvantages between groups'. A panel of experts questioned EDI's effectiveness. Warning that equality law was being misapplied in the name of meeting EDI requirements, Badenoch wrote a comment piece for the *Daily Telegraph* in which she was blunter in her assessment of the industry, calling it 'snake oil'. She wrote of a government minister who had recently found that the training materials for a departmental quango included references to 'outmoded concepts like "unconscious bias", and "white privilege", and used a picture of someone holding up a placard saying "white silence costs lives". All of this bunkum was contained in mandatory training for 1,400 poor souls whose primary job is to help further the government's economic agenda,' she lamented.

Badenoch continued to take advantage of opportunities to challenge the progressive orthodoxy. In mid-April 2024, Dr Hilary Cass, a senior paediatrician, submitted her final report and recommendations on how to improve NHS gender identity services for children. Cass, who had been commissioned to undertake this project by the NHS in 2020, concluded that the evidence supporting the use of puberty blockers and other drugs by under-eighteens was 'remarkably weak'. She said children had been 'let down' by the NHS. In a powerful piece for the *Sunday Times*, Badenoch added her own thoughts to the debate as she lambasted pretty much every institution in the country, calling them cowardly for failing to stand up to 'extreme gender ideology'. She complained, 'It has become almost impossible to question fashionable theories' and warned that 'dissent is treated as bigotry' as she said 'the underlying problem of ideological capture' had to be addressed. She went on:

> When ministers raise the alarm or intervene this is demonised by Labour MPs such as Yvette Cooper as engaging in 'culture wars'. For anyone wanting to imagine what a future Labour government might do, look at the behaviour of the party in Scotland who voted for the Gender Recognition Reform bill that would have allowed men into women's prisons and enabled rapists to legally change gender. That bill was only stopped by the direct intervention of ministers such as myself in Westminster with the support of the Prime Minister. Sir Keir Starmer would not have done the same.

As if on cue, the next day the ConservativeHome Cabinet league table was published. It showed that she had returned to the number one spot, confirming her status among activists as the most popular minister in government. The next week, in a show of independence, Badenoch was one of only fifty-seven Tory MPs to vote against the To-bacco and Vapes Bill – championed by Rishi Sunak – which seeks to outlaw anybody born after 31 December 2008 from buying cigarettes in Britain. It was a free vote, meaning the protocol of ministerial col-lective responsibility did not apply, and with Labour votes it passed by 383 to 67. Many Tories abstained or were otherwise unavailable to vote, but by actively opposing the idea – and putting herself in the same bracket as Suella Braverman, Jacob Rees-Mogg, Robert Jenrick and Liz Truss – Badenoch showed on the record that her dislike of banning things was genuine. She explained that she was motivated by the principle of equality under the law. She bought into the argument that the upshot of banning tobacco purchases in this way was that, in future, adults born just one day apart would have different rights. Enforcing the law would also be impractical, she said.

She echoed these sentiments shortly afterwards when speaking at an international financial services conference in London hosted by TheCityUK, explaining to attendees that her job often involves 'the killing of bad ideas', giving the example of mandatory ethnicity quotas. 'Regulation has moved from protection against fraud and systemic failure to everything from diversity to green finance, and this ever rising tide of micromanagement will not necessarily make us or the financial markets stronger,' she warned. She bemoaned another trend.

It worries me when I hear people talk about wealth and success in the UK as being down to colonialism or imperialism or white privilege or whatever. It matters, because if people genuinely believe that the UK only grew and developed into an advanced economy because of exploitation and oppression, then the solutions they will devise will make our growth and productivity problem even worse. It matters in other countries too, because if developing nations do not understand how the West became rich, they cannot follow in its footsteps. And it matters when, as your Trade Secretary, I go to the World Trade Organization conference negotiating on the UK's behalf, and some of my counterparts spend the entire time in meetings talking about colonialism, blame the West for their economic difficulties, and make demands that would make all of us – not just in this country, but around the world – poorer.

Few Tories would disagree.

By 2 May 2024, media predictions of Sunak's political demise had reached fever pitch. Some assumed – and with great relish in certain newspapers – that if the Conservatives sustained heavy losses in the local elections taking place in England that day, he would be ejected and a leadership contest would have to take place. This would mean the arrival of the fourth Tory leader and Prime Minister in the space of five years. On the eve of the poll, Badenoch was sanguine when asked about this possibility during an interview on Sky News, insisting that Sunak was safe regardless of the outcome and promising that he had her 'full backing'. To the surprise of few people, the Tories fared badly, losing 474 councillors and coming third behind Labour, which gained 186 councillors, and the Liberal Democrat party, which ended up with 104 new councillors. Valued Tory figures including Andy Street, the West Midlands mayor, also lost power that night.

No move against Sunak followed. Those who had been plotting against him were unable to muster sufficient support and gave up their hope of staging a coup. One unnamed rebel told the *Daily Mail*, 'We're off to the pub.' Then, on a rain-soaked 22 May, Sunak took the country by surprise by calling a general election. Standing outside 10 Downing Street in an increasingly sodden suit, he informed the nation that the poll would be held on 4 July. This left Badenoch, in common with every other member of the Cabinet who intended to stay in politics, to go out and start to campaign, in her case in the renamed seat of North West Essex, Saffron Walden having been abolished as a constituency after 102 years. Unlike most of her colleagues, however, the question in her mind was whether she would continue to serve under Sunak when the result was known or, in the event of the Conservatives losing, whether she might succeed him as party leader.

EPILOGUE

The Conservatives entered the 2024 general election campaign knowing that whatever the outcome, the party would never be the same again. The reason for this was simple. Before Parliament had even been dissolved, seventy-five of their MPs had announced that they were standing down, sweeping away a wealth of experience in one go. Of those who decided to defend their seats, many seemingly accepted that the Tories would lose power. They anticipated a much-needed phase of regeneration, starting with the replacement of Rishi Sunak as leader. Among the handful of candidates who might succeed him, Kemi Badenoch was widely tipped as the favourite.

Having spent months looking at Badenoch's life and career, and after ruminating on the words of her friends and colleagues, there is no doubt that she does want to lead the party. As one of her closest allies exclaimed the week before the election was called, 'She would *love* to face Keir Starmer.' The question is under what circumstances she would be prepared to take on what is usually described as the worst job in British politics. William Hague has referred to his four years facing Tony Blair between 1997 and 2001 as 'the night shift'.

Neil Kinnock once called the period when he opposed Margaret Thatcher and then John Major, between 1983 and 1992, 'purgatory'. Many challenges await the next opposition Conservative leader and the contours of the result will surely have a bearing on who would want to command those Tory troops still in Parliament after every vote has been counted on 5 July.

One longstanding political friend of Badenoch, Lord Lilley, is cautious. 'She could very well end up as leader of the party,' he says.

> Were Sunak to resign after the election, I personally think it would be a mistake for her to stand immediately because whoever replaces him may find they have to wait a while [to become Prime Minister]. The electorate tends to give governments at least two innings nowadays, though as it happens I can't think of any candidates who have more credence and credibility than her.

For different reasons, another distinguished Tory, who left the Commons in May 2024 after more than twenty years, also wonders if 2024 is too soon for her.

> Kemi has risen so quickly because she's prepared to say what she thinks. She's impressive and she could be a future leader, but the party has developed a bad habit of choosing people who are inexperienced. Mrs Thatcher had been an MP for sixteen years before she became party leader and [to me] that seems to be the gold standard.

There is a belief that Hamish Badenoch would have the casting vote on whether or not his wife put herself forward to succeed Sunak. A friend explains:

Hamish and she are like a team. He's an incredibly supportive political spouse: they met through politics, when they were both young activists, and he's always shared her view of how important her job is. He put her career ahead of his own. He is her political confidant as well as her husband. If he said to her that he didn't think her being leader would work for the family, she wouldn't do it. She respects his judgement perhaps more than anyone's and realises that what she does is a joint production with him. She's very family-orientated and spends as much time with her children as she can.

Even if her husband objected, however, a question that she would have to address in her own mind is whether the chance for her to lead would ever arise again. Political careers are shorter than they used to be. As somebody who went from backbench MP to Cabinet member in the space of five years, she would know that better than most.

Why would Kemi Badenoch want to be Tory leader? Several of those who have worked with her over the past couple of years have noted that she is driven to a large degree by a love of Britain and of the Conservative Party, which she has referred to as an extension of her family. 'When I listen to Kemi, a lot of her conservatism is based on having seen a different life and culture,' says Daniel El-Gamry, a special adviser.

Britain is meritocratic. She is deeply appreciative of that and she really does love Britain. She spent her first sixteen years under various socialist regimes in Nigeria. She would hate for Britain to go anywhere near that sort of situation. Much of her contemporary politics can be traced back to what she experienced there

– whether it's a commitment to free markets, free expression or free trade. In her office there's a picture of Roger Scruton's quote 'Good things are easily destroyed but not easily created.' That's what she believes.

Alex Burghart adds:

She doesn't take for granted what a lot of other people can take for granted about a first world country. She sees very clearly some of the things that are brilliant about the West and the UK particularly. That's refreshing in an environment when there are so many people talking everything down.

Another friend agrees.

Her experience in Nigeria informs much of her politics. Kemi is an immigrant steeped in African culture and I think her immigrant status is far more important than her skin colour. It means she is an African British woman. That has shaped her character. And she's got this Nigerian approach to conflict resolution. That's stayed with her. She will leap in. To her, this is all about combat. It's not about making or winning arguments, it's about fighting. It's about making enemies if she needs to. For her, politics has always been a lot more visceral. That comes from her upbringing.

On the assumption that she did stand, the first thing to consider is how she would fare in the contest. At the time of going to print, party rules required MPs to narrow the field to two candidates who then face Conservative members out in the country. Some say it is not a foregone conclusion that Badenoch would clear this first hurdle as easily as the bookmakers reckon. 'She's not as popular as she needs to be on the right of the parliamentary party,' says one party colleague. 'Some people feel she's quite aggressive and arrogant. I think she's quite confrontational, but in a good way because she doesn't mind taking people on. But – unless she's playing a clever game by showing independence of the right – she will need votes on the right of the party.' An ally says, 'She can be abrasive and perhaps she doesn't engage with her colleagues enough. But my observation is that if you're a 5ft 4in. Nigerian immigrant, you probably do have to have sharper elbows if you want to get to the top.'

If she were to make the final shortlist and face party members, a possible complication awaiting her relates to her enthusiastic membership of an administration that has presided over record levels of taxation and immigration. Would Conservative Party members object to her association with these policies – especially since at least one potential rival, Robert Jenrick, resigned from the government on a point of principle? Or would they look to the future and conclude that she is the politician who would pose the greatest threat to Sir Keir Starmer and a Labour government? Badenoch's colleague Julia Lopez subscribes to the latter point of view. 'She knows Labour would take the country in precisely the wrong direction and she would be great at interrogating those fundamental weaknesses,' says Lopez. 'She's not frightened to attack when she thinks things are wrong. I think she'd dismantle Labour and their corrosive brand of identity politics. Imagine the contrast – Starmer taking the knee after bowing to pressure groups, while our party makes Kemi its leader because of her intellect, courage and values.' Incidentally, she would also be the fourth female Tory leader since 1975. By contrast, there has never been a permanent female Labour leader.

Badenoch is certainly well liked among many grassroots supporters, as successive ConservativeHome polls show, and she is known to have been a popular speaker at association dinners since September 2022. What else, apart from eighteen months as a Cabinet minister and a persuasive speaking style, would equip her for the job of leader? Lord Maude, who is responsible for helping her get into national politics almost twenty years ago, is in no doubt. 'She's the standout candidate to lead the party,' he says.

> She's clever and brave and she has real star quality. She is deeply pro-business, which is an absolutely necessary condition for a Conservative leader. She understands it. If Conservatives don't make the case for business and capitalism, sure as hell nobody else will. She has smaller-state instincts and believes in families and communities getting on with things without being dependent on the state. She's in favour of lower taxes. I've always felt she was more socially conservative than me, and that's fine. It's when we get way out of kilter with the rest of the country that there's a problem.

Over the past fifty years, the big battles that have taken place in British politics have tended to focus on major issues such as monetarism and privatisation. In the Conservative Party, there have been arguments between wets and dries, modernisers versus traditionalists. As the second quarter of the twenty-first century begins, politics for many voters has become about their reaction to the state's tentacles reaching ever further into their lives, particularly in relation to 'woke' issues concerning race and gender. As this book has shown, Kemi Badenoch's voice has become a powerful and effective weapon in that struggle. But colleagues insist there is more to her than being a so-called culture warrior. 'She's conscious of not wanting to be seen as too hardline on some small "c" conservative issues,' says one. 'Her gang in Parliament are the clever, moderate right-wingers, not the Red Wallers. I think she's quite keen to be seen to be sophisticated in her politics.'

Badenoch has referred to herself as a 'classical liberal' in the past. One colleague says he sees her as a right-wing liberal. 'She's right-wing on the economy, law and order, immigration and all of those things,' says this person. 'But she's not a social conservative. She's not kept awake at night worrying about gay marriage, the family, mothers being at home and so on. She's a modern woman.' There seems to be no pithy label that can be attached to her. The Tory factions dubbed the 'five families' were backbench operations that she, as a Cabinet minister, had little to do with, but there is a consensus that she would not have wanted to belong to any of those clans anyway. She would rather have started her own grouping. Beyond her libertarian principles around free speech, her traditionalist approach to gender and race, her belief in enterprise and her hatred of living under a corrupt socialist bureaucracy, what else does she stand for? Lee Rowley insists she should become the next Tory leader because she is the only person who has thought properly about how the right should reinvent itself in a way that isn't superficial or oppositionist. 'Kemi and I agree there have been some good reforms since 2010 but nothing fundamental and consistent since the days of Thatcher,' Rowley says.

We're living off the reforms of our predecessors. We have to work out what reforms are necessary. Within government you can see the levers that worked in the '80s and '90s are furring up.

There's an element of the civil service tempted by activism and ideology, but more broadly it's a set of questions about activist lawyers, greater use of judicial review, inability to manage risk in public life. Very little of this came from explicit legislation but has built up, over the decades, through incremental changes or power transfers. In totality, it has made government less responsive and less close to ordinary people's lives. And, from a political perspective, the Conservative Party will need to rely upon a new coalition – put together over Brexit but needing lots of care and attention over several decades. Should a vacancy ever arise in the future, the party needs a leader who can set out our aims, explain how we'll achieve them, and communicate that effectively. No recent leaders have ticked all three of those boxes. Kemi comes closest to ticking all three. If the chance arises, she has an understanding of what's required.

Yet it is said by others that, as leader, she would need to rein herself in and pace herself. One seasoned Westminster observer who knows her well says:

She's humorous but she can also become quite passionate and that passion can become anger. She'd need to work on that. I think in future she could either save the country or she could self-destruct. Either outcome is equally likely. Speaking passionately and from the heart can be someone's undoing in politics. She's instinctive. Critics would say she can be impulsive. She has the potential to be a fantastic PM. Like Thatcher, like Churchill, she is driven by principle. People like that want to make a difference. But she could end up like George Galloway. Being driven by principle is no guarantee of success.

In keeping with this view, in interviews for this book some journalists made it clear that her relations with parts of the press have sometimes been tricky. She is not always regarded as the smoothest pebble on the beach. And she would need to change her attitude. 'She can tell people to get lost,' says one senior media player.

> Though less politely than that – and way more than you'd expect. She can find it really annoying and distracting to have what she regards as untruths written about her, even if they are quite trivial points. You find me a politician who hasn't been subjected to that! It's not that she's thin-skinned. It's that she believes in having debates and arguing things out. She needs to be able to let things go more. If you want people around you then you need to be able to forgive a lot more – a lot more than she does anyway. She's not a great one for turning the other cheek. She's more of an eye-for-an-eye kind of girl.

There is a belief that conservatism in Britain has reached a fork in the road and must rediscover its sense of purpose, much as it had to following the two electoral defeats the Tories suffered in 1974. Half a century later, the Conservative Party has become fractured. It needs to regroup and work out what its values and aims are. This may represent an opportunity for Badenoch. The fact that she is harder to place politically than some of her colleagues on the right could be to her advantage. She has certainly shown that she can be pragmatic rather than rigidly ideological – a feature that could count for a lot in a leadership election if a compromise candidate is needed.

Kemi Badenoch is one of the most interesting politicians of her generation. She has an electric quality, and an energy, that most front-rank figures in Westminster do not possess. There is also a sense of fearlessness about her that many voters find attractive. Some politicians find her courage, clear-thinking and confidence off-putting, interpreting it as arrogant or high-handed. Yet few would fail to acknowledge that these attributes have served other political leaders of the past admirably. They could work just as well for Badenoch in the future.

INDEX